BEYOND WAGE SLAVERY

Ken Coates

SPOKESMAN BOOKS

First published in 1977 by:
The Bertrand Russell Peace Foundation Ltd.
Bertrand Russell House
Gamble Street
Nottingham
for *Spokesman Books*

Copyright © Spokesman Books 1977

ISBN 0 85124 176 X
Cloth

ISBN 0 85124 177 8
Paper

Printed in Great Britain by
Bristol Typesetting Co. Ltd.
Barton Manor
Bristol

During recent years there has been a notable outbreak of democratic agitation, which has been noticeable in the Soviet Union, in the United States and in England. While the specific debates in which this reveals itself differ in origins and subject matter, there is a strong moral affinity between the various spokesmen who have become identified with it.

The brothers Zhores and Roy Medvedev, Noam Chomsky and Tony Benn, have, in the development of this argument, earned the trust of their countrymen and encouraged the hopes of a wider world which is sick with oppression and inhumanity.

To them this book is dedicated with profound thanks and warm affection.

Contents

Foreword

These essays represent part of a rather diverse output, which has included a lot of pamphleteering, some journalism, and a number of more sustained efforts to find some sense of direction, some orientation, in the confusion of prescriptions which has arisen during the great renaissance of socialist thought and advocacy which has burst into public attention during the past two decades. A previous collection, appearing under the title *The Crisis of British Socialism*, concerned itself with the day-to-day issues of the Labour Movement in Britain during the time of the Wilson administration of 1964-70. In this volume the essays are rather longer in their range and the arguments concern issues about which I would hope to be right, even if I were to be proved hopelessly wrong about the short-range options and instrumentalities.

It is my profound conviction that socialism will either represent the future democracy or else become a mere fantasy, a will-o'-the-wisp: while I am fearful that, without a thorough-going and radical socialist transformation of its structures, democracy will be unlikely to outlive the century. As Aneurin Bevan used to say, each freedom can only be made secure by adding another to it: while, we might add, there are still considerable forces at large in the world which will not feel secure until each of us is taught our place, and how to stay in it. Socialism would, I think, long ago have arrived, had it not allowed itself to be first divorced from, and then even counterposed against, democracy.

Today's world is divided between alleged democracies in which certain liberal freedoms have been uneasily preserved, in spite of mounting pressures to abate or restrict them in the interests of property; and alleged socialisms in which the smallest hint of creative dissent is rigorously choked by an aging and increasingly insecure bureaucracy. The established powers in each sector of the world have been compelled to try to live with each other by the fear of nuclear apocalypse, but the result is a twisted paradox in which each partially underpins the other. An English dissident democrat therefore feels keen affinities with his American or Soviet counterparts. In this context, West European socialism charges its batteries on the Prague Spring, while radical gains in Italy or France will unleash fierce popular turmoils in Poland or Hungary.

It is therefore beyond doubt that the central problem of worldwide socialism remains that of the discovery of a solid basis for socialist democracy. Since I began working closely with Bertrand Russell in 1965, I have had more than sufficient occasion to learn about the nature of repressions of various kinds in every corner of the globe, and a large part of my day-to-day work has been concerned with propagandist agitations arising from this dreadful knowledge. But it is vitally necessary to form conclusions of a more general and abstract kind than are involved in the simple defence of civil liberties. This collection suffers from the disability that it was written during stress, in moments snatched from day-to-day campaigns: so that it certainly will not represent the last word on any of the questions it considers. But I hope it may prove useful in winding together various strands of a vital argument, the opening of which is, at last, shaping up.

The individual essays which follow were first published in the following order: chapters one and eight were featured in *The Incompatibles*, published by Penguin

Books in 1967, and edited by Robin Blackburn and Alexander Cockburn; chapter two was a paper prepared for the I. G. Metall Conference on The Quality of Life in 1972; chapter three appeared in Peter Buckman's collection, *Education Without Schools*, published by the Souvenir Press in 1973; chapter five was the conclusion to the Spokesman book *Socialism and the Environment,* which I edited in 1972; chapters six and seven respectively were published in *The Spokesman* and *The Times* in 1976; chapter four was the introduction to *A Trade Union Strategy in the Common Market*, published by Spokesman Books in 1971; while the last chapter was a contribution to *The Socialist Register 1973*, edited by Ralph Miliband and John Saville, and published by the Merlin Press.

I am grateful to those who first gave each of these papers a public audience, and I am also profoundly grateful to Chris Farley, Ken Fleet and John Daniels, who have put up with me while I have been trying to puzzle out these heavy problems, and to all those students and colleagues who have tried, not always unsuccessfully, to save me from error.

1

Wage Slaves

More than thirty years ago, a sensitive adult educationalist published a series of extracts from the writings of his students about their attitudes to their work. These students had all been active trade unionists, men of above average resourcefulness and intelligence. Their accounts of the feel of factory life were uniformly forbidding.

A minder in a cotton spinning mill described his work:

'The mule is fed by boys and the process-work of turning the partly prepared cotton sieves into yarn is controlled by the spinner who is termed the minder . . . The machine dominates my work. I have to follow every movement of the mule, and as the speed increases so must I. If I leave the machine the broken threads accumulate and the mule must be stopped whilst the broken ends are pierced.'[1]

A colliery screen-hand wrote, in a distinctly familiar vein:

'Coal comes past me on an endless belt, and it is my duty to separate any dirt there may be from the coal. The belt sets the pace at which I must work. I have no feeling of power when working at the machine: on the contrary, I feel dwarfed, and I feel that the machine, instead of serving man, has become his master.'[2]

Another miner described his attempts to keep pace with underground machinery:

'One machine was vomiting more than I could clean up, the other had a larger mouth than I could fill. The outcome was a constant worry: I was working always at the top speed without any sense of rhythm. I often wished that all machines and the men who made them were in hell burning.'[3]

These workers all went up to Ruskin College in the early 1930s. One who completed the course there some time earlier was the engineer, R. M. Fox, whose description of his work, published in 1928, is still vivid:

'The invariable comment when the leaving-off hooter sounds is, "there's the one I've been waiting for all day!" And in the morning when the starting signal is given, they mutter "Roll on the second one!" They look forward every day to the end of so many hours of life. Such an attitude towards work cannot embody the final wisdom of the ages.'[4]

This picture is one which I understand from the inside in a rather particular way: long before I ever meditated on it, I had become accustomed to the greeting which all Nottinghamshire miners exchange every morning: "How are you?"—"I'll be all right on Friday!" After nine years of such a customary greeting, I went to university. For several weeks I astonished students who asked me how I was by informing them that I would be all right on Friday. It was with a real sense of realisation that it dawned on me one day that Friday was no different from any other day in my new calendar, where freedom ran all through the week. This experience helps to persuade me that things are not so different today, and that the industrial regime of the 1960s is much less of an advance upon its forerunners than most public relations men are prepared to admit.

In 1965, another worker, from a tobacco factory, on

his way up to Ruskin, wrote an article for *New Left Review* just before he moved :

'. . . The other day I overheard two old employees who had been in the factory to receive their pensions. They greeted each other as I passed. "How's it going, Bert?" said the first, "Lovely, Bill" the other, recently retired, replied. "Anything's better than that bloody hole." This may seem a paradoxical reference to a place where someone has spent forty years of his life . . .

'It is probably wrong to expect factories to be other than they are. After all, they are built to house machines, not men. Inside a factory it soon becomes obvious that steel brought to life by electricity takes precedence over flesh and blood. The onus is on the machines to such an extent that they appear to assume the human attributes of those who work them. Machines have become as much like people as people have become like machines. They pulsate with life, while man becomes the robot. There is a premonition of man losing control, an awareness of doom. The machines seem to squat restless in their oily beds awaiting the coming of some mechanical messiah . . .

'Sometimes I have an urge to open the nearest door and walk and walk and walk. I feel a need to get away from this atmosphere of here and now, where all that matters is the present, good or bad, and one must make the best of it. Nobody desires change. Everybody is looking into an endless flat future and thinking they could be worse off.'[5]

Of course, all this is impressionistic evidence. It is also tiresomely familiar. Satanic mills have been part of our landscape since the industrial revolution itself, and the romantic protest against them, however one-sided and utopian it has sometimes been, has provided a fearsome documentation. The alienation of this Nottingham

tobacco worker was pinpointed by Herman Melville over
a century ago, with his piercing if now depreciated meta-
phor of the cogs:

> 'Machinery, the vaunted slave of humanity, here stood
> menially served by human beings, who served mutely
> and cringingly, as the slave serves the sultan. The girls
> did not so much seem accessory wheels to the general
> machinery as mere cogs to the wheels.'[6]

The condition has also been thoroughly and blister-
ingly documented in the first volume of Marx's *Capital*.
More recently it has been analysed and broken into
a whole range of potentially accessible problems by
Friedmann, while it has given rise to fierce complaint by
the founder of cybernetics, who devoted a whole book
to:

> 'a protest against the inhuman use of human beings'.[7]

It is hardly curious that clever and perceptive workers
continue to write this sort of description of their lives,
registering their humanity in their protest against the 'inhuman use' which is made of them. From time to time
their complaints are heard by investigating sociologists;
the problem of alienation, often somewhat hazily appre-
hended, is becoming increasingly frequently discussed by
academics. What is strange is that there also exists a
general and dominant mythology which hinges on the
official belief that, with 'affluence' and modern man-
management, this kind of difficulty is under control, and
that factories have been transmuted into a new style of
living. These complaints, for all their undeniable onesidedness, indicate very plainly that in spite of half a
century of declarations that Labour 'has ceased to be a
commodity', the moral status of workers today is in no
fundamental sense different from what it was a hundred
years ago, while *Das Kapital* was still being read in

galley-proof. Naturally, these harrowing commentaries by escapees from the mesh of factory life do not accurately represent the whole of it: it would be fair to say that even in the most estranged environment workers will discover some way of being involved in their work, some small sense of achievement, however attenuated, covert and harassed. What these repeated cries of pain indicate is that the *normal* condition in industry is one of semi-captivity: that inside the prison an occasional bird may sing is not denied.

In any case, individual descriptions of the feel of work are by no means the only evidence about the situation of labour in modern Britain. Lord Robens recently complained that voluntary absenteeism in the mining industry had reached 5.77 per cent of the industry's available man-power, equivalent to a permanent labour force of 27,000 men or an annual £46 million of output. And, in a controversial statement, the Chairman of the National Coal Board also queried the stringency of the criteria used by local practitioners for certifying sickness, on the grounds that involuntary absence has reached new heights. (If there is a heaven to which miners sometimes gain admission, undoubtedly it will include a little window on to purgatory, in which will be labouring, with exemplary fortitude and minute punctuality, all the unlamented legions of Coal Board bureaucrats, productivity-hounds and Labour politicians who ever incited other men to still further intensify a dreary toil which they would not, on Earth, even dream of taking, however lightly, and however temporarily, on themselves.)[8] But the collieries are not the only enterprises from which work-people temporarily absent themselves.

Over industry as a whole, sickness absenteeism has been steadily increasing during the past ten years. More than 300 million days a year are now being lost by employed men and women. Particularly important is the increase in psychoneuroses and psychoses. This, for male workers, rose from 13.2 million days of certified incapacity in the year 1953-4, to a provisional estimate of 17.66 million days in 1963-4. The rise in accident rates was even greater, from 12.66 million cases to 18.8 million during the same period. Other, physical, sicknesses have also tended to take a heavier toll in recent years. Dr. Beric Wright, commenting on these facts, points out that:

'all over the world, absentee rates are going up more or less parallel with the growth of social security benefits and hospital services. This overall increase cannot be entirely due to previously untreated disease. We ought as a nation to be fitter than we ever have been, but we are spending more and more time away from work.'[9]

Dr. Wright goes on to advance a diagnosis which is entirely relevant to our argument:

'The problem . . . is not one of disease, but of lack of job satisfaction and motivation . . . This becomes clear from the study of the typical businessman. It might be assumed that he can afford to be ill and take long holidays. But the survey carried out by the Institute's (of Directors) Medical Centre showed that directors average between two and three weeks' holiday a year. Some take a month, but overall they do no better than their staff. And they certainly work longer hours. The Medical Centre now has three sets of figures about sickness absence . . . these show that, including *all* long- and short-term sickness, the average director loses only between four and five days a year. Over 60 per cent of directors go for years without losing any time at all . . . Their sickness rate is about a third that of the rest of the working population.'[10]

Something should be allowed for the fact that directors are their own masters, and can moderate the burdens they lay on themselves when they feel out of sorts, which their employees cannot do. We can allow a little more for the fact that there may be grounds for including under the heading 'work' for directors such burdens as business lunches, sundry rounds of golf, and various other chores which other people might regard as play. On top of this there is the far more telling fact that directors usually vet and submit their own reports on their own activities, a boon not granted to lesser men, whose activities are reported on by others, often without their being given access to the results, and sometimes without their even knowing that reports are being made. Even so, Dr. Wright's argument is not so far-fetched as many workers might think it. 'The more responsible a job, the more strongly motivated its holder, and the more persistent his work', runs its thread. The story is plausible. True, Dr. Wright goes on to attempt to square the circle, by insisting that 'Governments must govern, managements must manage, and everyone needs to work'. The obvious cure for endemic malingering, if the doctor is right about the example of the directors, would be to distribute their mana of responsibility far and wide throughout the populace, in the hope that strong motivation and the virtues of persistence would be distributed with it. Instead, Dr. Wright thinks it necessary to concentrate power, and presumably with it civic and industrial virtue. Yet in spite of this foible, the rest of the diagnosis makes sense. What is remarkable is not that things are as he says they are, but that anyone should expect them to be otherwise. Rational employees might be expected, on working out the balance of advantage, to become disciples of the Good Toiler Schweik, inveterate and skilful malingerers to the last man. The wonder is not that some do, but that most don't. If responsibility carries with it commitment, helotry produces withdrawal: and when Dr. Wright appeals for the sharpening of managerial authority, the

stiffening of the division of function, he is in fact appeal-
ing for an intensification of the very problem he is trying
to solve.

Sickness is by no means the only avenue through
which the frustrations of factory-life may be partially
eased. There are innocent escapes, like day-dreaming and
the football pools. There are also more violent solutions.
One of these is little-documented, but, I suspect, significant. It consists of individual sabotage. A worker who is
hard-pressed by the speed of his machine may find a way
to cause it to stop. The first time I observed this happening I was a boy in a colliery in the Midlands. I was sent
to a conveyor-head on the coal-face which was rather
difficult to operate, since the seam through which the
face was running was very thin and rather badly faulted.
I arrived to find a lad sitting by the gear-head, wielding a
seven-pound hammer. He had stopped the belt from running, and was carefully whacking at the metal stitches
which joined two long sections of belt together. Raw, I
asked him what he was doing. 'Won't that break the
belt?' I said. 'What the hell do you think I'm trying to
do?' he replied. When the conveyor in this seam broke, it
did not assure lads like this belt-driver of an easy time.
Far from it. They had to race about up and down the
face, snaking on their bellies all the way, and working
much harder than usual. The boy was registering his
protest against boredom, he was getting some of his own
back on the machine which dominated him, and he was
demonstrating his indispensability to the colliers down
the face who normally took his efforts for granted.

In all these integrated protests the psychologists who
study small group behaviour might labour for months to
find a co-ordinated pattern of response. But there is one
central question which needs to be asked: why did he
not contemplate the feelings of the manager who was
striving to raise output, or of the Coal Board who were

currently trying to beat a fuel crisis of major proportions, or of a government which was trying against odds to restore a shattered economy which still rested on coal? To ask it is to dismiss it. It is safe to say that these important matters never even entered his head. Why should they? Who could truthfully say that they were problems in which he had even a fractional interest? By sabotaging all these worthy drives, this one boy was making his own life more difficult, but more interesting. Doubtless a delinquent solution. But how many millions of such delinquent incidents are there every day in British industry? Sabotage of this kind, it should be emphasised, is purely an individual reaction. There have been times when sabotage has been used as a collective, trade union, weapon: notably the Luddite episode. It was an integral weapon in the syndicalist arsenal, both in the shape of temporary or permanent disablement of machines, in the broadcasting of discreditable commercial secrets, and in the practice of ca'canny and obstructionism. But in his book, *Strikes*, G. C. K. Knowles argues, rather convincingly, that it 'generally characterises a weak trade union movement, where . . . it is difficult to prevent the use of blacklegs or to maintain a long strike'.[11]

Paradoxically, a principal obstacle to personal withdrawal of these kinds is precisely the development of solidarity among the workers. This also takes place as a reflex response to their treatment in this alienated environment. Not only do the loyalties which workers form to one another greatly reduce absenteeism and increase the degree of attention paid to mutual tasks and safety, but often men have found ways to relate themselves to what they have rightly regarded as a hostile society, precisely through the institutions which they have formed to protect themselves from it. If one examines the progress of such fierce rebels as Ben Tillett, John Burns, Ernest Bevin, and Ray Gunter, from subversive fire-raisers and rabble-rousers to establishmentarian reconcilers, dousers of conflict, disseminators of official pieties, one can quickly see that it has only taken place through the medium of solidary opposition, which has been contained within the hostile social structure. Unions have formed not only a front-line defence against the regime of alien-ation and exploitation, but also a bridge from the con-dition of withdrawal to 'involvement' in a controlled way in the policing, for Authority, of what is for it a funda-mentally lawless territory. They are thus inherently am-bivalent.

During the early years of the postwar boom, which effectively disoriented a whole generation of leading socialist propagandists, it was popular to assume that the attainment of full employment had solved all the basic problems which have been traditionally posed in socialist discussion. As C. A. R. Crosland has put it:

> 'The status of the worker, in any sense, has been rather substantially enhanced as a result of full employment, rising real wages, social security legislation and a general change in the social climate ...'[12]

Within this view of things, not only had poverty been dissolved, but 'democracy and social justice' were on their way. For Crosland, the principal significance of the problems we have been discussing would be the evidence that they offer of lack of 'job satisfaction'. He would tackle them on two levels: on the low range by 'improv-ing the standard of personnel management,' and as a longer-range goal by 'unravelling the natural group re-lationships' at work in order to 'align these with the tech-nological necessities of the work process'. This bizarre devaluation of the problem is a classic example of what Marx would have denounced as 'commodity-fetishism'. Rather than align technique with human needs, Crosland's crude and philistine approach is inevitably the reverse; it does not envisage for one moment a *human* society in which things serve people. But even Crosland is prepared to admit the historical concern of socialism with this goal:

'Historically, the aspiration towards a "juster" organisation of industry has been enshrined in the demand for industrial democracy and workers' control. This has a long history in the Labour Movement . . . reaching a climax in the stormy decade before the First World War when even revolutionary syndicalism briefly caught the imagination of the British unions; while Guild Socialism, a more prudent and pacific version, took a strong hold on the minds of younger socialist writers . . .'[13]

However, Crosland by no means infers from this that 'justice' might require that attention be paid to these pioneers: on the contrary:

'If we wish to revive this issue, we shall not derive much help from the old literature . . . (it) was ideologically rooted in a theory of "wage slavery" *which has no relevance to present-day conditions.*'[14] (my italics)

It is in the light of this comfortable conviction that much of the debate which has troubled academic sociology, concerning affluence and the changing class structure, has been conducted and as a result has been incapable of revealing much more than surface platitudes. 'A washing machine is a washing machine is a washing machine,' David Lockwood has written. His words might with profit be branded upon the rumps of most psephologists and a good many political commentators.

The relationships between employer and worker which the first Guild socialists described as 'the bondage of wagery' has not in the least been ameliorated by motor cars and refrigerators. On the contrary. While no one

would deny that there has been an absolute improvement
in the standards of living of workers in all the advanced
capitalist countries, which has continued throughout most
of the past two decades (and which has only been arrested
during the epoch of advanced, modernising technical
innovation inaugurated by Crossland and his colleagues
when they assumed poltical office), the important thing
is that this absolute improvement has not been ac-
companied by any significant *relative* improvement in
the rewards of Labour as opposed to those of Capital.
What really matters in evaluating this situation is not
simply the yardstick of comparative consumption, which
is often misleading. The key to an understanding of the
psychology of industry is the yardstick of comparative
accumulation, or agglomeration of *power*.

The original Marxist conception of exploitation never
concerned simple money robbery; it always involved
itself with the alienation of the product of labour from
the control of the labourer, in which workers produce,
over and above their own livelihoods *at whatever level
of 'affluence'*, a volume of capital, which, under alien
direction, concentrates ever greater economic force against
them in ever fewer hands. Conceived in these terms,
'exploitation' has been continuously intensified and aggravated throughout the whole history of capitalism.[15]
The growth of scale of modern industry is clearly con-
joined with the distillation of corporate political and
social power, which has not been diminished in any way
by 'high', or near-full employment, wage-levels. Decision-
takers, deriving steadily augmented authority from direct
and indirect titles to capital, cluster in a tightening throng
at one pole of society; at the other pole are massed the
vassals, who, in spite of the fog of a vast ballyhoo of
cynical devices for 'participation' or 'involvement', feel
the continuous pressure of attempts to cut back, erode
and remove any traces of real rights which they may have

been able to grasp at their own immediate level, over the
shaping of their own tasks and direction. Of course trade
unions have been able to seize some serious powers at the
workshop level, over working arrangements and the disposition of the labour force, during the intensive competition for labour which has persisted for most of the post-
war period.[16] But these powers, of which shop stewards
are rightly jealous, are under constant fire from authority,
both in management and the State at large. And while it
would be quite wrong to minimise the strength and self-
confidence of the trade unions in this persistent struggle,
it would be absurd to overlook the fragmentation which
has been induced in their ranks by the same economic
and political processes. If they were consciously bent
upon the destruction of the power of capital, the trade
unions could find means to accomplish it: this no one
doubts. But within the higgling of contending interests
inside the present power-structure it seems absurd to
speak of 'trade union power' in the same breath as the
power of capital. In the past few years the monolithic
National Union of Mineworkers, with near thirty members of parliament, including a number of ministers, and
under a Labour government upon which it has a thousand claims and ties, has found it impossible to secure
the fulfilment of the wholly specific promises it had been
given before victory in the elections. A sympathetic
Minister of Power recently burst into tears at a confrontation between trade union and government spokesmen,
but grim and implacable behind him sat Mr. Douglas
Jay, the voice of the Treasury and the bankers.[17] When
all the miners in the land weigh less than a handful of
bankers, it is premature to assume the rout of management prerogatives.

Both C. A. R. Crosland and H. A. Clegg, who have in
numerous books and articles celebrated the virtues of
permanent trade union oppositional power, have during

the Wilson administration been lending every possible practical assistance to the crusade to roll these powers back.[18] The inconsistency in their behaviour reflects a deeper inconsistency in their ideas. These ideas found a popular expression in Michael Shanks's account, *The Stagnant Society*, which was, in the terms of this kind of literature, a bestseller. In retrospect it may be thought that Shanks not only puts a key part of the Crosland-Clegg view into a nutshell, but also provides a convenient epitome of the basic industrial relations assumptions of the Labour Government:

'There is no greater morale booster for a worker than the feeling that he too is consulted on policy questions and plays his part in influencing managerial decisions. Of course, in any form of democracy there is an element of humbug. Our rulers never, in fact allow us as much power as they pretend to. The sovereign people can only be permitted to exercise its power on certain limited occasions and within certain defined limits—otherwise the operations of government would be paralysed. Nevertheless, the illusion of power is good for us, besides imposing important restrictions on our rulers.

'This applies to industrial democracy, where the element of make-believe must of necessity be greater than in political democracies. Because of the highly technical nature of the decisions which have to be taken, the management must retain ultimate control of the policy. Moreover, the analogy which is often drawn between industrial and political democracy breaks down on two vital points. The first is over the diversity of aims. Ultimately, we all have a common interest in the survival of our political community. But in a factory this may not be so. Only the employer has an interest in preserving the factory at all costs—and even he may be anxious to sell out. But the workers' interests might well be best served by increasing wages and decreasing hours of work to the point where the concern might be driven bankrupt—provided there were other jobs in the district for them to go to.

'This brings us to the second reason why industrial democracy cannot be equivalent to political democracy. The political rights of the individual in society derive largely from the fact that he is compelled to live in it. But the worker in industry can always 'vote with his feet' by moving to another factory. The unit of society, in other words, is not all embracing. This means that the worker cannot with justice claim the same rights *vis-a-vis* his employer as he can as a citizen *vis-a-vis* his government.

'Industrial democracy, in other words, is a matter of tactics rather than of high principle. It is in no sense immoral to run one's business as a rigid autocracy— but it is probably foolish. It is equally foolish, however, to surrender one's ultimate power of decision to a group of workers, or even to all the workers. Industrial democracy cannot be like a two-party political democracy, in which today's opposition may be tomorrow's government. In industrial democracy a permanent administration confronts a permanent opposition—and as everybody knows, in parliamentary terms this is a most healthy situation. To look at this matter sensibly, we would do well to forget all about the mother of parliaments and the far-flung analogies of the pundits, and consider the issue on its merits.

If one is to talk sensibly of industrial democracy then the first thing is to deflate it and empty it of ideology. It is the fact and not the form of consultation that matters.'[19]

Of course, in this passage, Shanks ducks all the main

problems. He outflanks his opponents by a simple device: he narrows the base of his model of industrial democracy to the point where it becomes possible to derive a whole series of completely discrepant analogies. The real unit which socialists aspire to democratise is not, as he is claiming, the factory. It is the economy. If it is true to say that members of a factory can 'vote with their feet', and most of us would claim that that was only true within very straitened limits, then the proper answer to this is that within his own analogy people who don't like Wapping can go to Broadstairs. (With similar difficulties, be it added.) The moment one begins to argue about 'society' the parallel area of dispute becomes the economy. It is absurd to pretend that members of 'the economy' can leave *it* any more easily than they can leave 'society'. If the State marks out the frontiers of 'society', then, to be sure, it is easier by far to leave society than the economy, for the very good and simple reason that not the State but the market marks out the shape of economic frontiers. In this case the reverse of Shanks's argument is true: it is far more easy for English feet to vote for Australia or Japan than to vote their way out of the economy. To argue for democratic control of the economy is not to argue against factory democracy: factories could and should be democratically administered. But to establish norms of workship democracy in an uncontrolled and undemocratic economy is to conduct a permanent Canute-like dialogue with the ocean of the market. Sometimes the tide will conform to our desires. The important times are those when it does not. Every day, mild fluctuations in demand wreak havoc in existing traditions of factory organisation. It is only if the economy at large is *both* planned and democratised, that the extension of democratic forms to the workshops has any permanency. As far as the Shanks argument is concerned, factory democracy can be vulgarly related to democratic central planning much in the same way that, within his own inadequate analogy, local government might be related to national government.

More woefully ill-founded though is Shanks's conviction that, in the sense that the opposition can never be allowed to win, there can be no two-party democracy within an industrial democracy. If the controllers of an economic plan are democratically controlled, they must be subject to organised criticism, backed by a free press and the liberal standards of open comment. If they are so subject, the possibility cannot be excluded that they might be displaced. In any of the existing centrally planned economies one cares to think of, it is fairly plausible to assume that some, at least, of the planners *would* be displaced if effective popular controls of this kind were established. Whether a democratic plan would necessarily require two or more institutionally established parties it is difficult to say in advance: no such plan exists as a convenient model. Probably its norms would require more of an unleashing of shifting but articulate caucuses and lobbies, forming and reforming according to the emergence of new social needs and pressures. These themselves would engender successive controversies and then settle them as they arose. But none of this is what Shanks is talking about, I will be told. Precisely. When he appeals for this whole problem to 'be deflated and emptied of ideology', those reading him might be tempted to offer a quiet 'Amen'. The fact, is that his whole assumption, that 'a permanent administration confronts a permanent opposition' in this best of all possible worlds, is completely ideological, in the precise traditional meaning of the word. *Why* can our industrial controllers never be displaced by popular vote when their policies cause disquiet? Because they are appointed to and fixed in their positions by the institution of property. Property alone within the structure can displace them, yet it is so

much of a taboo that in this vital discussion it cannot
even be mentioned. Every single form of rebuttal of
democratic arguments which is now being deployed
against trade unionists demanding real extensions of industrial democracy could equally have been, and indeed
probably was, invoked by the squirearchy in its staunch
resistance to the most elementary democratic demands
within the political field.

This complex of arguments forms a pattern. The orthodox 'revisionist' critics of socialism (who have cap-
tured at any rate the industrial relations policies of the
Labour Government) have been from the beginning prepared to recognise widespread alienation, which they
have seen purely as a psychological condition, a form of
individual withdrawal.

They have indeed been prepared to appropriate as
their own the call to 'radically improve the status' of the
working population, and to 'transform the quality of industrial life'. But they have diagnosed the condition
simply as a response to modern technologies, without
seriously considering how such technologies came to be
enforced, and what conditioned their employment. It has
always been assumed by them that it is 'natural' for
people to adapt to the requirements of the market in this
field. In the words of Brecht, their failure has been a
refusal to

> *Inquire if a thing be necessary:*
> *Especially if it is common.*

Had they been able to do this, they might have even gone
on to learn

> *When a thing continually occurs*
> *Not on that account to find it 'natural'.*

Implicitly accepting an impermissible framework for their
judgements, they can only seek limited solutions to global

problems. They are, for instance, prepared to explore all kinds of experiments in factory group dynamics, in order to adjust workers' errant minds to the mechanical imperatives against which they rebel.[20] Just as social psychologists during the war were able to employ group discussion techniques in order to brainwash housewives into feeding their husbands with offal, so this school of thinkers posits a labour force realigned, in small chunks, to a severe appreciation of the need for more production and its own self-abnegation. This is what Crosland means by 'alignment with the technological necessities of the work-process'. To help sell this placebo, labels like 'industrial democracy' can be applied to it. As Shanks revealingly confesses, this involves multiplying 'humbug' by 'make-believe'. But there is a limit to the potency of group manipulation, and the problem, truly posed, has never been one of how people may adapt to machines in the abstract. It has been one of adapting to *someone's* machines.

To explore what this means, consider two greenhouses. One, in a back garden, contains a happy fanatic who saved money to build it and now spends every spare minute nourishing tomatoes which he could possibly buy cheaper in the market. While he is in this greenhouse, this man would probably describe himself as 'free'. Yet he is certainly 'working'. The other greenhouse is one of a long row in a nursery. Two labourers pass on the way into adjoining doors. 'Roll on Friday' we hear them saying. Our particular man enters his work-place where we observe that, after carefully scanning around him, he settles comfortably down, and falls to the reading of the *Daily Mirror*. He is not working, but he is 'at work', and would certainly prefer to be reading the *Daily Mirror* elsewhere. He is behaving in an alienated manner. But can we say that greenhouses are alienating? Of course not: our first man cannot spend long enough in them. He

is his own master. The other two are working for someone else. Ignore this simple fact at peril: for the whole
essence of the alienation we have been describing is that
property, the private control of public resources, is at the
heart of it. Of course, greenhouses can be personal be-
longings. In this they differ from, say, a four-million
pound production-line in a vehicle factory which can
never, for any of its individual operatives, become really
'my' machine. But such a costly complex *could* become
'our' machine, and if it did, this would merely bring the
juridical norm into line with what has long been a social
need. Until this happens, every factory is a flagrant
assault on the categorical imperative: 'I ought never to
act except in such a way that I can also will that
my maxim should become a universal law.' If those
words were to be enforced in any working enterprise for
half an hour, it would cease to function altogether. Socialist revolutions in full flood apart, capitalist industry is the
most sustained and awe-inspiring collective effort which
men have ever made: yet its ethos is such that members
of the collective only traditionally use the words 'we' and
'us' when they are making hostile demands upon its
directors.

None of this is to say that all forms of work will become pleasant once we nationalise the means of production, distribution and exchange. The contrary: their very
unpleasantness, in a really open democracy, will hasten
the social effort to abolish them. The effort to do this has
always been seen by socialists as involving a double onslaught: efforts must be made to plan a technological
explosion, capable of blasting out continuous all-round
cuts in working hours; at the same time there must also
be a systematic transfer of increasing ranges of consumer
goods to welfare forms of distribution, gradually but
remorselessly replacing money as the normal means of
personal transactions, and increasingly relegating it to

the role of an accounting device between various public corporations. The effect of these onslaughts would be a vast increase in *free time*, which, in such conditions, as Marx frequently pointed out, 'is the *most productive* time of all'. This, in turn, would lethally undermine the division of labour itself, which has hitherto given rise not only to the impositions of class and rank, but also to the conditions which Ruskin so tellingly described:

'We have much studied and perfected, of late, the great civilised invention of the division of labour; only we give it a false name. It is not, truly speaking, the labour that is divided; but the men: divided into mere segments of men—broken into small fragments and crumbs of life; so that all the little piece of intelligence that is left in a man is not enough to make a pin, or a nail, but exhausts itself in making the point of a pin, or the head of a nail. Now it is a good and desirable thing, truly, to make many pins in a day; but if we could only see with what crystal sand their points were polished—sand of human soul, much to be magnified before it can be discerned for what it is—we should think there might be some loss in it also. And the great cry that rises from all our manufacturing cities, louder than the furnace blast, is all in very deed for this—that we manufacture everything there except men; we blanch cotton, and strengthen steel, and refine sugar, and shape pottery; but to brighten, to strengthen, to refine or to form a single living spirit, never enters into our estimate of advantages.'[21]

Ruskin may have approached this terrible reality in a one-sided manner, but at least he faced it. Our present generation of 'socialist' leaders do not even know what it is about. They may have thought about it, briefly, once; and in mitigation we can accept that to deal with it no doubt requires a fairly long-range strategy. They are all

B

busy people. However, not thinking about these long-range problems makes the range still longer, and the haul uphill still harder.

By foreshortening its range and lowering its aim, Labour in Britain has set a cruel trap for itself. Immediate, 'practical' problems have for so long dominated the minds of the Labour establishment that they have no independent criteria by which to respond to them. No one in the present government has time to think about the overcoming of the division of Labour. But if no one thinks about such matters then the goals of the movement become devalued. For all the loud noises we have had from Labour leaders about 'equality' over the past fifteen years, every evidence appears to show that this notion is strictly limited to piety of a most abstract kind. The complete failure of any prominent spokesman of the Labour Party to discuss this kind of problem in fundamental terms, during the whole of the past two decades, reveals a definitive retreat from the most crucial front in the battle for Labour's aims.

This refusal to think about these ultimate problems blocks Labour leaders from opening up the vision of the members of the movement. At the same time it forces them to accommodate to a position in which their short-range moves are completely blind. They come to rely entirely on the given priorities of the established system. And so, they come to reduce all political choices to administrative alternatives. In this way, the 1964 Labour Government found itself with the strategic aim of 'restoring the economy'; after which (in some way which has neither been specified nor, one suspects, agreed) 'we will pay ourselves a dividend'.[22] Instead of becoming the reason for beginning to create a new one, the difficulties of the old economic order became a pretext for placing in jeopardy even the limited programme of amelioration which had previously been envisaged. Not only has the incidence of poverty been increasing, but there are signs that this is happening at an accelerated rate. Professor Townsend, who calculated recently that some $7\frac{1}{2}$ million people were living at or below the standard available on National Assistance, is now publicly speculating about the increase of this figure by another million. In this serious condition, the policies of retrenchment which have been imposed upon the administration add their own quota of misery. The deliberate creation of artificial unemployment, referred to under the repulsive name of 'shake-out', marks out the ultimate capitulation to the logic of the market, to the primacy of property over all humane interests.

A man's hopes are his moral boundaries. He will rarely press beyond them. If someone merely aspires to put a new roof on his kitchen, not only is it easier to fulfil this dream than to bring about a world in which *every* cook may learn to govern the state, but, when the roof is on, you will not find prime ministers in the kitchen by accident. In the event, in 1964, even the kitchen roof could not be seen to. Worse. Having accepted the administrative priorities, the restoration of the old order to good health required the new ministers to make incisions in the economic body. Cuts could not be inflicted upon capital's prerogatives without stepping outside the administrative routine which had by now become more demanding with each submission made to it. And so arose the need for first piece-meal, and then wholesale attacks on the living standards and liberties of the very people the Government had been elected to protect.

The word for this is 'betrayal'. It is an emotive word, but, unfortunately, it is accurate. Yet the first and fundamental betrayal took place a while ago, almost unnoticed: it was a betrayal of socialist theory, since which the events 1964 and onwards have only made manifest something which was gestating, latent in a small flow of books and articles, for a decade and half before.

Having inherited the leadership of a vast mass organisation of working people, the present dominant caucus
had not the remotest idea of an aim for the whole complex. Because their horizons were so limited, they reacted
like any sealed-in provincial village community, and
embellished their own immediate social arrangements
with polite and decorous descriptions to soften the realities. In the village everyone will tell you that much
can be improved, that no one is complacent, that many
reforms are needed, and so on. Similarly Mr. Crosland
was in favour of uplifting the status of the workers, just
as Mr. Shanks would spread more widely the humbug of
democracy, just as all the world and especially Mr.
Harold Wilson would love to blow warm blasts of modernising wind through every enterprise. But workers are
not merely deprived of status by some genteel scale.
They are, as every line of this essay is meant to argue,
wage slaves. There can, if this is true, be no easy continual uplift of the people without a fundamental structural change in society as a whole. A wage slave does
not cease to be a wage slave when he can buy a refriger-
ator. Roman slaves might be thin or fat, sad or cheerful,
employed to entertain their masters' lions as dinner or
their masters' wives as lovers; wage slaves too come in all
sizes and conditions. Some even drive to work in motor
cars. As they trod the grape harvest, the Roman slaves on
the *latifundiae* probably ate some too. You cannot tell a
wage slave by his looks. You can tell him by the fact that
on Monday he says 'Roll on Friday'. He is defined by
the fact that he lives in little islands of freedom called
'leisure'.

These, to an outsider, may be more and more
resemble the surrounding sea of 'work' is not
ng. It is hard to be a five-day slave, free at
Recently in the same week, I visited a phar-

maceutical factory employing some thousands of girls, and a fun-arcade at Skegness. In both places, rows and rows of girls stood poring over rows and rows of little machines. The first enterprise was for bottling, sealing, and labelling pills; engaged in it the girls were 'producing'. At the second, which was for taking away the sixpences earned in the first, the operatives were 'consuming'. Work and leisure, production and consumption: fully *human* beings would have to reason with subtlety to discover the difference. Wage slaves know it intimately; it is the first fact of their existence. If wage slaves who earn above average pay feel the freer for that on Friday night, they will most probably feel all the more enslaved on Monday morning. A Derbyshire colliery under-official won £20,000 on the football pools two years ago, and having assembled a fair-sized crowd in the pityard, he ceremonially burnt his pit-clothes in front of them. They knew what he meant.

*   *   *

In sum, if slavery is a social relationship and not an absolute level of distress; and if slavery may be discovered wherever the will of one man is involuntarily and arbitrarily subordinated to that of another; then we remain bound to the same basic problems which the Labour movement faced, one hundred years ago, when Marx offered it this excellent advice:

'At the same time (that they defend themselves with vigour in all partial battles for improved conditions) . . . the working class ought not to exaggerate to themselves the ultimate working of these everyday struggles. They ought not to forget that they are fighting with effects, but not with the causes of those effects; that they are retarding the downward movement, but not changing its direction; that they are applying palliatives, not curing the malady. They ought, therefore, not to be exclusively absorbed in these unavoidable guerilla fights incessantly springing up from the never-ceasing encroachments of capital or changes in the market. They ought to understand that, with all the miseries it imposes on them, the present system simultaneously engenders the material conditions and the social forms necessary for an economic reconstruction of society. Instead of the *conservative* motto: 'A fair day's wages for a fair day's work!' they ought to inscribe upon their banners the *revolutionary* watchword "For the abolition of the wages system!"[23]

First published in 1967

FOOTNOTES

1. A. Barratt Brown, *The Machine and the Worker* (London, 1934), p.85.
2. ibid.
3. ibid, p.86.
4. R. M. Fox, *The Triumphant Machine* (London, 1928), p.35.
5. D. J. (Dennis Johnson), 'Factory Time' in *New Left Review*, 31 (1965), pp.51-7.
6. Herman Melville, *The Tartarus of Maids* in Collected Short Stories (London, 1950).
7. Norbert Wiener, *The Human Use of Human Beings* (Boston, 1950).
8. An honoured place among these toilers will be reserved for Harold Wilson, who will need a fair slab of eternity to demonstrate how easily he could dispense with 'conservatism' on the shop floor in order to boost the dynamism of British Industry. It is perhaps unfair to predict that Purgatorial Industry may also slacken its pace when it comes under his inspired tutelage.
9. 'The Sick Society', Dr. Beric Wright, in the *Director* (October 1966), pp.90-1.
10. ibid, p.92. For an account of the Report of the Institute's Medical Centre see the *Director* (May 1966), p.270ff.
11. G. C. K. Knowles, *Strikes* (Oxford, 1952), p.13. The best known advocate of sabotage as a trade union weapon in this country

was William Mellor, cf. the appropriate chapter in *Direct Action* (1920). Recently the idea has been discussed in the militant journal *Solidarity* in somewhat similar terms. Since this essay was written a major study of *Sabotage* has been written by Geoff Brown (Spokesman Books, 1977).

12. C. A. R. Crosland, 'What Does the Worker Want?' in *Encounter* (February 1959), p.10.

13. Crosland, *The Future of Socialism* (London, 1956), p.343.

14. ibid, pp.343-4.

15. Those who doubt this interpretation of Marx should carefully re-read *Wage Labour and Capital*. An extract may serve to point his attitude both in the field of consumption and accumulation:

'A house may be large or small; as long as the surrounding houses are equally small it satisfies all social demands for a dwelling. But if a palace arises beside the little house, the little house shrinks into a hut. The little house shows now that its owner has only very slight or no demands to make: and however high it may shoot up in the course of civilisation, if the neighbouring palace grows to an equal or even greater extent, the dweller in the relatively small house will feel more and more uncomfortable, dissatisfied and cramped within its four walls.

'A noticeable increase in wages presupposes a rapid growth of productive capital. The rapid growth of productive capital brings about an equally rapid growth of wealth, luxury, social needs, social enjoyments. Thus, although the enjoyments of the worker have risen, the social satisfaction they give has fallen in comparison with the increased enjoyments of the capitalists, which are inaccessible to the worker, in comparison with the state of the development of society in general. Our needs and enjoyments spring from society; we measure them, therefore, by society and not by the objects of their satisfaction. Because they are of a social nature, they are of a relative nature . . .

'Real wages may remain the same, may even rise, and yet relative wages fall . . . If, therefore, the income of the worker increases with the rapid growth of capital, the social gulf that separates the worker from the capitalist increases at the same time, the power of capital over labour, the dependance of labour on capital, increases at the same time.'

from *Selected Works* (London, 1945), vol. 1, pp.268-73.

16. For a balanced treatment of this, see Tony Topham, 'Shop Stewards and Workers' Control' in *New Left Review*, 25 (May-June 1964), pp.3-16.

17. cf. *The Scottish Miner* (February 1966).

18. Compare Clegg's discussion of these matters in *A New Approach to Industrial Democracy* (Oxford, 1960) with his part in framing the Devlin and Pearson Reports on the decasualisation of dock

        workers (Cmd 2734, August 1965) and on the Seamen's Wage
        Claim (Cmd 3025, June 1966).
19. Michael Shanks, *The Stagnant Society* (London, 1961), p.160-1.
20. Crosland, 'What Does the Worker Want?' loc. cit., pp.16-17.
21. Ruskin, *The Stones of Venice*, Section II, chapter vi.
22. As James Callaghan pointed out to the Fabians at a gathering
        during the 1963 TUC: 'A Labour government must not rush its
        fences . . . its first job must be to get industry moving again (!).
        Then we can start paying ourselves a dividend' (*Guardian*, 4
        September 1963).
23. Karl Marx, 'Value Price and Profit' in *Selected Works*, vol. 1
        (London, 1945), p.337.

2

Industrial Democracy and the Quality of Life*

Arguments about the quality of life in industrial society have recently taken on an urgency and stridency which, if belated, is none the less welcome to all who have a lingering fondness for mankind. As our air is poisoned, our rivers and seas made sterile, or worse, virulent with hostile elements, our countryside desecrated and our very future as a species put in doubt by the profligate consumption of such all too finite resources as remain available to us, so, somewhat after the eleventh hour, we begin to complain. It is right to try to save the environment. Yet the one virtually infinite resource which mankind possesses is that of *human* potential which is most stupidly, and most cruelly, thwarted by the present rapacious economic order, at whose door most other complaints against pollution of both nature and society must also be laid.

The founder of cybernetics, Norbert Wiener, was keenly aware of the waste of human capacity involved in modern industry.

The German metalworkers' union, I.G. Metall, convened an international seminar at Oberhausen, on 'The Quality of Life', and this paper was delivered there.

The ideas contained in it are the product of extensive discussion with my colleagues of the Institute for Workers' Control, and notably with my co-author, Tony Topham. The argument is developed at greater length in our book The New Unionism, *published by Penguin Books in 1974.*

'In my mind' he wrote 'use of a human being in which less is demanded of him than his full stature is a degradation and a waste. It is a degradation to a human being to chain him to an oar and use him as a source of power, but it is an almost equal degradation to assign him to a purely repetitive task in a factory, which demands less than a millionth of his brain capacity. It is simpler to organise a factory or a galley which uses human beings for a trivial fraction of their worth than it is to provide a world in which they can grow to their full stature.'[1]

But the 'full stature' of a human being is a developing stature, in which intellect, passion and will are all free to assert themselves. Wiener's cry of pain for the people who are mutilated in our society is in no way novel, and has antecedents in moral philosophy which date back at least as far as the thought of Immanuel Kant.

The dictum of Kant 'always treat humanity in your own person and in others as an end and never as a means', merely holds out a criterion for human behaviour which, while it retains its appeal, is quite clearly inoperable in our society. All economic activity, all productive organisation in capitalist industry is based upon the systematic violation of the categorical imperative. In every factory, mine, office and government department we find that men and women are compelled to labour to realise goals which have been determined by others, to augment the power and prestige of others, to enrich others and enlarge their influence and status. Employees are not merely subordinates: they find their subordination intensified by the fact that their interests and aspirations can be imposed or manipulated by social forces quite beyond their individual or collective control. Most workplaces do not even leave their work-people free to fix even their own speed or rhythm of toil, while often even their pauses and rest-breaks, postures and work-dispositions are externally, and all too arbitrarily, determined. Legions of workers are driven deaf by noise-levels which are insupportable by normal human beings, or have their sight impaired, or suffer physical mutilation by the inexorable side-effects of industrial processes. It is impossible for those who administer this state of affairs to claim that the maxim 'do as you would be done by' is even remotely applicable to their conduct.

Yet the opponents of this state of affairs are in no stronger position to act upon the Kantian prescription than those against whom they react. Trade unions and political parties, if they operate within the established structures, must strike a daily progression of compromises with those forces which are based upon the use of men as objects, as tools in some greater purpose of capital aggrandisement. Even those who reject the given system completely, and opt for its revolutionary overthrow, can have no immediate use for Kant. They require to establish counter-institutions, an alternative division of political and military labour, in which it is quite impossible to treat every man as 'an end in himself'. This fact was recognised by Trotsky, who wrote:

'A means can only be justified by its end. But the end in turn needs to be justified . . . and the end is justified if it leads to increasing the power of man over nature and to the abolition of the power of man over man.'[2]

The English sociologist Ginsberg[3] saw this notion as purely Kantian in its scope. However, there are good grounds for judging it to be quite different from Kant's injunction: it is applicable to our present problems, while Kant's is not. By introducing a distinct component of relativism, and by transferring its prescription from the present (as edict) to the future (as ultimate aim), Trotsky sets out a line of march, rather than an initial commandment. But such a line of march can be pursued in different formations, at different speeds, and with means by no means uniform with those Trotsky felt to be imperative. The struggle to overcome the power of one man over another will certainly recur in capitalist industry: it has by no means exhausted its impulse, and to think that it could cease would be to imagine that humanity was capable of choosing helotry at a time when its technical capacity for freedom had never been greater. What is clear, however, is that struggle will take experimental forms, as it has throughout the whole history of the Labour Movement:[4] that it will essay a whole variety of initiatives, learning all the time that it acts.

In this sense, the movement for workers' control of industry is profoundly revolutionary, even while it pursues the most limited reforms. At the same time, if any socialist movement represents the continuation, development and realisation of the basic liberal criteria of democracy, it is this one, because it is impossible to agitate for the growth of democratic forms complex enough to govern the enormous scope of modern industry without comprehending every significant lesson which has been learnt in the parallel, but simpler, struggle to impose accountability upon the governors of political institutions.

Quite clearly, it is absurd to speak of real democracy, of real accountability, in institutions which are dominated by property. In today's industry, a handful of owners not merely command obedience from a vast mass of employees, but have so arranged affairs that the most active productive efforts of their subordinates can only intensify their dependence.[5] The greater their productivity, the greater the augmentation of hostile powers which may be used against them, even to the point of their own displacement from labour itself. The reality of this process has been made abundantly plain in Britain, where in recent years, between 1963 and 1971, indices of employment have moved from 100 down to 94.5, while those of productivity have moved from 100 up to 117. Not to put too fine a point on matters, the associated labours of workpeople in Britain have thus produced an alien power which has precipitated something like one million of their brethren out of work altogether.[6] Unfortunately, this story repeats itself in other countries wherever the same conditions apply. Even when operating at its most efficient optimum levels, capital can only intensify the subordination and degradation against which Wiener was raging. The signs today seem to be that this optimum, with its concomitant 'affluence' is in increasingly acute peril. No doubt this partly explains the renewed interest in socialism and in industrial democracy.

Advocates of industrial democracy fall into two species. There are those who either wish to embellish a fundamentally undemocratic structure with decorous descriptions, or who are gulled into accepting such pretences for reality. And there are those who wish to socialise private property in productive organisations, and to extend to industry the same presumptions which are alleged to govern political institutions in the most advanced capitalist democracies. The first category speaks a great deal about 'workers' participation in industry' without ever impinging on the hard realities which impel workers *not* to participate. Their strategems were summarised in the wallposter which appeared in Paris during the 1968 upsurge:

I participate
Thou participatest
He participates
We participate
You participate
They profit

The second category do not usually speak about 'participation', although when they do, they mean something

more than subordinate consultation. They usually speak
of 'workers' control' as their prescription for the erosion
of arbitrary power in plant, industry and economy in
capitalist society, and of 'workers' self-management' as
their goal for a socialist society.[7]

Of course, this terminology is by no means universally
accepted, so there remain possibilities for semantic disputes. On one side, workpeople are apt to take the
promises of 'participation' or 'consultation' seriously, so
that frequently demands which might legitimately be
characterised as claims for more control are made under
the formulae of insistence upon 'fuller participation' or
'proper consultation'.[8] At another extreme, some socialists use the term 'workers' control' to describe their norms
for the administration of socialised economies, and simultaneously decry the more conventional trade union demand which organises itself around the same slogan, as
at best a palliative, at worst a delusion.[9] Yet there is very
considerable evidence that various controls *can*, within
limits, be encroached from the unilateral disposition of
management by alert trade unions in certain favourable
conditions. Of course, all free collective bargaining denies
unilateral managerial control over wages, hours, and certain types of working conditions. But in every advanced
western European country some trade unions have gone
far beyond imposing such elementary restrictions, to establish varying degrees of control over hiring, firing, training, speeds and dispositions of work, health, safety
regulations and their enforcement, and in some cases,
over access to accounts and apposite financial information
concerning the prospects of the firm.[10] In many cases,
legal powers for limited controls may be secured by trade
union political pressure, as in the notable instance of the
legally established workmen's inspectorate in the British
coal-mining industry. It should be stressed, however, that
all attempts in Britain to extend similar powers to workers

in manufacturing industry, or even to employees in the notoriously dangerous deep-sea fishing fleets and the merchant navy, have so far proved fruitless.

In the words of Hugh Scanlon, President of the British engineers' union, the AUEW;

'There already exists, particularly in fully unionised concerns, a considerable degree of workers' control in individual factories, if "workers' control" is defined as effective control by organised workers over the arbitrary powers of management. This is indeed "the seed of the new society inside the old". Shop stewards prefer, and seem to get more out of, workshop bargaining than the type of "consultation" favoured by management . . . This radical move away from the defensive mentality of the past is graphically shown in the fact concerning the causes of industrial disputes. It has been shown that between 1940 and 1960, the proportion of strikes (excluding strikes in the mining industry) not directly concerned with wage-increases, but connected with disputes such as those about working arrangements, rules and discipline, have risen from about one-third to three-quarters of the total. In 1960, a TUC survey showed that only 32% of strikes were directly about money: 29% were about dismissals alone. In this brief survey it is clear that the changes in the Labour Movement since the 'thirties are making nonsense of the concept of a purely 'economic man', limited to actions in defence of his standard of living. Far wider issues are involved today.

'Yet even the extension of the current type of "workers' control" can be seen as holding only a watching and limiting function on the "rights" of management. Workers are demanding an *effective* voice in management policy. This aspiration is particularly concentrated in regard to the nationalised industries, where obviously the greatest scope is offered to the demand that management be obliged to obtain the consent of workers in all matters of industrial policy. Trade unions envisage a radical extension of the scope of collective trade union action, from a point beyond wages and salaries to human conditions of employment in their broadest aspects.'[11]

Similar views have been expressed by many British Trade Union leaders, notably Jack Jones,[12] the secretary of the largest union in Britain, the Transport and General Workers' Union; Ernie Roberts, the Engineer's Assistant Secretary; Alan Fisher, the Public Employees' leader, and spokesmen of the Post Office and Technicians' unions.[13] Demands along the same lines are particularly evident in the agendas of some of the most dynamic white-collar unions, where physical proximity to managerial personnel and close familiarity with some of the crucial problems involved in decision-taking clearly have no noticeable effect in damping the appetite of employees for a non-servile status.

This current of thought is by no means confined to British labour. Perhaps the most coherent statement of trade union aspirations for industrial democracy, and the most integrally thought-out strategy to achieve such aims is to be found in the programme which was adopted in 1971 by the Belgian Socialist Unions, organised in the General Federation of Belgian Workers*.

Naturally, the tug-o'-war involved in 'encroachment' of this kind is by no means a one-way affair. When conditions are ripe for employers to act, they will attempt to erode the powers temporarily ceded to their workpeople. In every West European country, when employers have lost too much ground to the unions, there have been attempts at political intervention to subordinate the

* See below, pp.72-74.

unions to governmental regulation. Perhaps the most graphic instance to date of such intervention is the British Industrial Relations Act of 1971, which attempts to weaken the powers of unions at the shop-floor level by a variety of expedients. At the moment of writing, the TUC is resisting the enforcement of this law by a general policy of non-co-operation, and its effect must therefore remain subject to doubt, real though its intentions certainly are. Whether the unions will be able to frustrate those intentions by withholding co-operation remains to be seen.

Yet throughout the political turmoil in which this Act was produced, and during the whole length of the discussion of its provisions in Parliament, the struggle for the extension of trade union control powers was continually developing in Britain. To take one example: the Confederation of Shipbuilding and Engineering Unions repudiated a procedural agreement which had been imposed on their industries ever since the 1922 lock-out of Engineering workers. In negotiating for a new set of procedural arrangements, they insisted that any change whatsoever initiated in working conditions by management should, before implementation, be subject to criticism and objections from the shop-floor, and recast in their light. That is, the *status quo* must apply during all such negotiations. Obviously, this has significant implications for workers' control at plant level, for it implies that the workers would have the right to veto the unilateral and arbitrary decisions of management over a wide range of issues—dismissals, redundancies, discipline, alterations in speed and content of work, manning arrangements, and so on. The *status quo* demand, which received the backing of the TUC in 1969, is a crucial practical way of strengthening plant level workers' control, and goes a long way towards disentangling shop stewards and unions caught up in the meshes of post-productivity bargaining 'participation'.[14]

To take another example: in the fight against unemployment, which passed the half-million mark in the middle of the term of office of the Wilson administration, and has since risen continuously to its present level, not only have trade unions continued to recruit additional members from a declining labour force, but quite novel forms of struggle have been devised to defend work-opportunities. The most famous of these is the 'work-in' of shipbuilders on the Upper Clyde,[15] in which general subscriptions by the labour movement have enabled the relevant shop stewards' movement to maintain on a trade union payroll, large numbers of workers declared redundant by their bankrupt firm and so to effectively veto their employer's 'right' to dismiss his staff. Work-ins are only possible where the nature of the work involves long-term construction projects, and attempts to imitate the Clyde action in the motor cycle factory of BSA in Birmingham were a failure. But similar actions at Sheffield Steelworks were highly successful. Another Scottish plant which was 'closed' by the Plessey telecommunications company has been occupied by its workers ever since: and the example of this 'sit-in' has had a widespread effect. The outbreak of such struggles has had a particularly galvanising effect upon employed workers in Scotland, surrounded as they are by extremely high levels of male unemployment.[16]

Building on these examples, as we have explained at greater length elsewhere,[17] shop stewards and rank-and-file trade unionists become increasingly concerned to elaborate strategies to erode managerial monopolies of information, which are traditionally defended under the appeal to business secrecy, and to create powers of *representation, veto,* and *supervision* over production decisions in general, as well as those concerning employment.

'In order to safeguard gains made in this way, the active trade unionists have to work hard to improve democratic relations between themselves, the members they represent, and the union to which they belong. Reporting back procedures, and the right of members to call their delegates and representatives to account, and to dismiss them if necessary, are all vital insurances against the dangers of rank-and-file union incorporation into management's ethos. The other crucial requirement for advance is that national and local trade union centres gear themselves to effectively service the shop floor initiatives.[18] The whole strategy of encroaching control requires a big expansion of trade union education, and of research and accountancy services which are both available to trade unionists, and at the same time accountable to them. If the union bargainers at plant level are really to make a challenge for access to, information on, and powers of veto and supervision over, the employers' investment plans, they need to acquire self-confidence in handling a whole new range of ideas and facts. All the experience of adult education confirms that workers are of course perfectly capable of acquiring this self-confidence if they obtain the opportunities to do so. But plant bargaining, and plant-level controls over procedure, are not enough. They are the base on which much wider frames of reference may be built. If workers do not look beyond their own plants, their view will inevitably be a narrow one. On the crucial question of employment opportunities and redundancies, the trade union side in plant bargaining finds itself compelled to take a wider view than that dictated by the immediate short-term interests of those workers in the plant who will be retained in work. Even when "no redundancy" promises are made, the goal of modern management is normally *saving on labour cost*, and this may be

achieved in the context of improved productivity by
natural wastage, retirement and labour turnover. The
result is, of course, that job opportunities for new
entrants into industry are reduced, and overall unemployment rises. It is very difficult to see this perspective
solely from the plant; if, however, a District Committee of a union, or a Trades Council, did some arith-
metic and added together the loss of job opportunities
from labour-saving agreements made in the major
plants in their locality, the point would quickly be
appreciated.'[19]

In this way arises the question of the need for a trade
union 'social audit'. Giant steps forward in this direction
were taken during the Upper Clyde dispute, when the
Scottish TUC initiated a full scale enquiry into the social
costs of closure of a major part of the Glasgow shipbuilding industry. This enquiry summoned vital witnesses, and met for nine days under a considerable blare
of publicity in the Scottish press. The Institute for
Workers' Control submitted important evidence on the
scope of a 'social audit',[20] and testimony was taken not
only from economists and experts on shipbuilding, but
also from planners, welfare workers, and other persons
with knowledge of the total social effect of the closure
decision. In a number of other disputes which have taken
place since the Scottish enquiry reported, workers have
proposed similar public investigations, in which employees of universities and other public bodies have will-
ingly participated.

In all these examples, it is clear that the detailed work
of defining the meaning of workers' control is very much
a task for workpeople themselves. When one comes to
look at the problems of socialist societies, and the demand for self-management of both industry and plan,
this is no less true.

Workers' control, as discussed above, however aggressively pursued, expresses a series of basically negative democratic restraints upon the exercise of authority in industry. Taken to its ultimate conclusion, it does certainly raise the question of new forms of social ownership and democratic administration. But the establishment of such new forms is a political labour, which, however it is accomplished, will necessarily amount to a social revolution. Models for self-management in such a new society clearly require not only to establish sound criteria for social planning and industrial development, but also to relate these to real criteria for full democracy in decision-making at every level, which cannot possibly exist without the widest freedom of criticism, openness of the press and communications media, and freedom of political association.

Since societies which call themselves socialist are often rather backward in encouraging democracy of any kind, leave alone self-management, it is still necessary to look at the arguments for self-management in relation to the experience of workpeople in the advanced capitalist democracies.

'No man is good enough to be another man's master' wrote the English socialist William Morris. But in a world in which masters dominate, the social arrangements over which they preside are so arranged as to obscure its truth. Myths are created, with the prime object of justifying the right of rulers to rule, owners to own, managers to manage. These myths cannot succeed in their prime object, however, if they do not, at the same time, achieve a secondary effect: the undermining of the self-confidence, critical judgement and independent initiative of all those over whom rule is exercised.[21]

This is a common story. In the United States black people have been dominated, ever since the overthrow of direct slavery, as much by their own carefully implanted sense of inadequacy as by the force at the disposal of authority. When Malcolm X and his friends began to preach 'Black is beautiful', and the movement for Black Power started rolling, the first and key element in the upsurge of the black population was a new self-recognition. Black people had to recognise themselves, but they also had to learn to like what they recognised. In the same way, the movement for Women's Liberation has to begin with an attack on all the complex attitudes *held by women* which contribute to their subordination. And with the working people, things are not fundamentally different. Whilst workers take for granted their right to political suffrage, they are prevented, by attitudes which pervade their whole upbringing, from conceiving industrial suffrage as natural or just. The first and main protectors of arbitrary authority in our society are not the public guardians of law and order, but the policemen who operate in the heads of the people who are held in subjection. What are these mental policemen? In the old days there were savagely distorted religious ideas, which not only placed God over Heaven just as the King ruled the State, but went farther, to uphold the notion that the King derived his own authority directly from God, to whom alone he was accountable. If there are modern workers who believe in God, there are few among them who would be prepared to accept that He appointed the Chairman of the Board of Directors, and fewer still who see the lineaments of divinity in the inconsiderate and impolite fellow who, all too often, is entrusted with the immediate supervision of their work. More subtle myths, rationally founded, are required to justify the present industrial order.

We must necessarily examine two of these. The first is the myth of 'intelligence'. Some men, we can all see, are cleverer than others. You have to be clever to run a factory. If you are clever, provided you're not *too* clever, you'll get on. All these common-sense perceptions have now been systemised into an extensive theory of intelligence, which, however often it is questioned or discredited, still persuades many people that they are too stupid to know how to conduct their own collective affairs. The theory, in its crudest form, states a number of propositions. One is that intelligence is a quality which is secreted in individual heads. Another is that the capacity to secrete it is determined genetically, so that it can be inherited. A third used to be that this capacity was fixed, and unchanging, so that it could be objectively measured by an intelligence quotient. An extension of it, commonly made, is the fourth proposition that people in subordinate roles occupy them because they are inadequate in intelligence, and could not do otherwise than they are doing. All four propositions are questionable. We would be wise to regard intelligence as a social product, resulting from the social interaction of people. Whilst all kinds of characteristics can be inherited, most people who are not mentally handicapped—in a strictly medical sense—are capable of learning up to the highest standards, provided that the learning starts early enough, that the teaching is effective and that the process is not subject to counter-influences from the labour market, which discourage the learner and distort the role of the teacher. Because it is a social development, the capacity of people to show 'individual intelligence' is very variable indeed, and can be drastically affected by changes in the social environment. And people in subordinate roles occupy them because people who aren't in them like to keep things that way.

Yet it remains true that workers need to learn much before they can manage their own factories. If learning facilities were made available to them by the factories, they could acquire the right knowledge relatively simply. But factories are organised in ways which prevent them from being taught, so that the whole process of management appears to be out of reach.

The second myth is that property is the whole basis for a free society. This myth used to be a great deal truer than it is today. In the Middle Ages, when 'town air was free air' and the guilds were at their height, a workman would own his tools, his shop and his product. Apprentices would learn their skills and subsequently become masters. Property in scissors, needles and cloth was indeed the very foundation of the freedom of the tailor, or the glover, in such a society.

But the property in the vast concert of machines which are currently working towards the manufacture of the RB 211 aero-engine is a very different story. Those who own this equipment can only do so at the expense of the freedom of all those who have to work it. Unless this ownership becomes truly social, that is to say communal, it is bound to restrict the general freedom, not advance it.

None of these arguments prevents many workers from seeing things differently. If you ask ten engineers at random whether they believe in, say, the socialisation of the engineering industry, at least three or four of them will say 'No': and when pressed for a reason, answer 'How would you like it if you worked all your life to build up a sweetshop, and the Government came along and took it?' Of course, sweetshops aren't aircraft industries, and might well be left for ages to the control of individual shopkeepers, who might, indeed, feel the freer for the fact. But when workers make this equation, which is wrong, they do so because it corresponds to the 'normal' assumption of the culture they inhabit. It is 'normal' for factories to be privately owned and autocratically managed. It is 'natural' for workers to be allocated to jobs which do little or nothing to develop their capacities, and subjected to disciplines which are calculated to restrict their initiative to minimal levels. If these things are usual, then they all too easily become accepted as un-avoidable and, even when resented, may well be seen as, in some sense, 'fair'.

Yet the idea that no man is good enough to be another's master constantly recurs. It can be traced throughout the history of industrial capitalism, from its very dawn. The goal of social self-management has never really been purged from the body of the trade unions, or the political parties of Labour. With every crisis of the established order, it is wont to reappear. It is repeatedly announced to be dead, outdated or primitive. Men who have re-nounced it repeatedly secure preferment after the fact. Its partisans are frequently reviled and sometimes per-secuted. Nonetheless, it keeps coming back, and has done so ever since the beginning of socialism.

This vision has been expressed with considerable clar-ity by Hugh Scanlon, in words which do much to reveal the quality of the new generation of trade union leaders which is emerging in Western Europe.

'One cannot give any kind of detailed blueprint for such a radical transformation as a transition to a socialist society under full democratic workers' self-management; what we can do is to analyse certain tendencies and safeguards that can be the basis of pro-posals to map our route without falling into the twin traps of local free-for-alls and excessive centralisation. Certainly with nationalisation, workers must not be made to feel, as they certainly do at present, that there is only a political change while there remains an indus-trial status quo. Fundamentally, the aim within public ownership is the wearing down of sides in industry, with no "superiors" or "inferiors" but only differences and functions based on knowledge and ability. Only through public ownership could there be this real will to co-operate.

'There need be no real contradiction between the necessity for integration and centralisation of resource planning in a modern developed economy, and a structure of democratic decision-making that allows flexibility and the development of local initiative. It seems a false assumption to counter-pose the two. Indeed the decentralised "market" criteria of the Yugoslav pattern constrain the workers' freedom in work (irrespective of works-council decisions) and hamper the development of the economy. A caricature of a market economy cannot give workers effective decision-making powers over an economy. At the other extreme, a "national plan" run purely by a small circle of bureaucrats at the top as well as being unacceptable to the democratic aspirations of the British labour movement, is also economic nonsense in an advanced, highly complex industrial system. The consumer, although having no formal industrial rights, has a vital part to play in exercising controls over prices, quality and choice. Indeed the election of consumer committees at all stages of price and production determination would help to direct industry to the service of the community.

'A central planning medium needs the democratic participation of works committees and consumers, as well as specialist advice. Communication in industry in national, as well as plant planning, is a necessity. Ideas, aspirations and intentions need to have full access and be encouraged upward, whilst explanations, snags and problems should be moved downward for discussion and the creation of an informed working populace. The works' committees, rising through industry to national planning need the safeguards of full political democracy in order to discuss and decide upon alternative plans for economic and structural development. Even where there is full workers' control in the industrial plants, workers will be left in a purely passive executive position if they cannot effectively discuss, and draw up the central plan itself, and have the opportunity to modify or change it in tune with changing circumstances or needs. Here the element of flexibility becomes all-important.

'There must obviously be a recognition that specialists would play an important, and possibly more vital role under a structure of workers' self-management. Staff appointments, carrying such duties as design, experiment and research would remain with a high degree of autonomy in their research. Managers with over-all operative duties could work under the guidance and eventual control of representative bodies of workers, holding the power of appointment, promotion and dismissals. Every workshop or department could elect, by secret ballot, representatives to deal with managerial functions and in turn consult frequently with workers. Large factories might require inter-departmental committees, but for smaller plant, the next stage would probably be factory administration. Administration would embrace different functional divisions, comprising members of primary committees together with consumers. Administrative factory committees could be endowed with power to select managers who in turn would appoint supervisory grades, at least in the initial stages. Representatives from Factory Committees, elected to Industrial Councils could be enabled to work out policies relating to the whole industry, and provide a link with other industries and planning authorities. The necessity for control must be balanced by the freedom which enables individuals to apply their own ideas, while keeping in mind, and making allowances for, the wider needs of the community.

'It has often been argued that a centralised planning medium of this character will inevitably lead to a new

ruling caste of managers and bureaucrats. This is obviously a point that needs to be carefully examined, in
particular to see what safeguards, both organisation-
ally and inherent in the structure of the society itself,
would militate against this. Obviously the maintenance
of political freedom to democratically discuss conflict-
ing views of planning would be a powerful safeguard.
But this by itself is not enough. The trade unions' role
in a nationalised economy can also be an important
factor in this direction. There is an essential need to
preserve trade union independence. The unions must
not be directly involved in controlling industry. The
value of the unions will lie in their ability to take independent action to redress industrial grievances and
act as a media for protection against injustice. Even
in the content of a plan, there is scope for unions to
act as bargaining agents and to play a role in determin-
ing wages.

'Institutional checks can be introduced to halt any
tendency towards an irresponsible bureaucracy. The
right of recall of representatives by the membership
and the interchangeability of positions, would go a
long way in this direction. However the main check to
the growth of administrative autonomy by specialists
would be provided by the benefits of a socialised economy itself. It has always been a basic socialist thesis
that a planned economy would lay the basis for a
tremendous increase in material resources, leaving
room not only for a swift reduction in the working day
(with the use of automation) but allowing, on the
foundations of rapid economic growth, for a great extension in educational facilities. Obviously one cannot
induce democratic involvement in industry by a stroke
of the pen, but an effective participation needs a tech-
nologically educated workforce. One cannot afford to
examine the viability of workers' self-management in a

static sense; technological advance could more than be equalled by cultural advance through the growth not only of administrative experience but of vastly improved educational resources. A reduction in the working day to allow time for study, would greatly accelerate this process.'[22]

The possibility that such changes in our industrial order may be accomplished is a very real one, which no-one should imagine to be utopian. If anything, such a transformation is overdue. It will not solve the many outstanding problems of our age, which require an end to underdevelopment in a majority of the nations of the world, and quite new approaches to the exploitation of the human environment. But in moving towards a liberation of all the talents which have hitherto been thwarted and oppressed in industrial civilisation, it will at least open up the opportunity for men to create a world fit to live in, and a style of life which they need not be ashamed.

First published in 1972

FOOTNOTES

1. Norbert Wiener, *The Human Use of Human Beings*, Boston, 1950, p.16.
2. Leon Trotsky, *Their Morals and Ours*, Pioneer Books, New York, 1968.
3. Morris Ginsberg, *Evolution and Progress*, Heinemann, London, 1961, pp.252-3.
4. We have documented some of the wide variety of these firms as exemplified in the recent history of the British labour movement, in K. Coates & A. Topham, *Industrial Democracy in Great Britain*, MacGibbon & Kee, London, 1968 (subsequently issued in a paperback edition by Panther books of London and then in four volumes by Spokesman Books.

5. For a discussion of the English evidence on this matter, see Michael Barratt Brown: *The Controllers of British Industry*, in *Can the Workers Run Industry?*, ed. K. Coates, Institute for Workers' Control, Nottingham, 1968. Also Robin Murray two articles in *The Spokesman*, Nos. 10 and 11, 'The International Company' and 'The State and the Internationalisation of Capital'.

6. John Hughes: *Behind the Dole Queue, The Facts about Un-employment*, Spokesman pamphlet No. 23, 1971.

7. For an extended discussion of these problems, see my *Essays on Industrial Democracy*, Spokesman Books, 1971.

8. As has been explained by Ernie Roberts in *Workers' Control and the Trade Unions*, published in *Can The Workers Run Industry?* loc. cit.

9. The 'palliative' view has been expressed by some leading British communists, and can be found discussed in *The Debate on Workers' Control* published by IWC, Nottingham, 1970. The 'delusion' view has been strenuously argued by certain Marxist-Leninist (Maoist) leaders in Britain, notably Mr. Reg Birch, in the journal *The Worker*, October, 1970.

10. Some of the evidence on these matters is to be found in the study by Coates and Topham: *The New Unionism*, Peter Owen, London, 1972, Penguin Books, 1974.

11. Cf. Hugh Scanlon: *The Way Forward for Workers' Control*, IWC, Nottingham, 1971.

12. Cf. Jones' contribution to the Labour Party debate on industrial democracy, in Coates, Barratt Brown and Topham, *The Trade Union Register*, Merlin Press, London, 1969.

13. The British postmen have long preached a doctrine of workers' control, and have in fact published a number of pamphlets on the question ever since the heyday of Guild Socialism in the immediate post-war years after 1918. The reorganisation of the post office under the Wilson administration brought about an ex-change of recriminating polemics between the responsible minister and the UPW, on precisely these questions. Cf. *Bulletin of the Institute for Workers' Control*, Vol. 1, 1968.

14. Although negotiations between the CSEU and the Engineering Employers' Federation have broken down, leaving the industry with no nationally agreed procedure for handling disputes, none-theless the unions are actively pursuing local agreements with such employers as are ready to settle, all of which must be based upon the acceptance of the 'status quo' principle. Cf. Coates and Topham *The New Unionism*.

15. Cf. the following publications of the Institute for Workers' Control: Eaton, Hughes, Coates: *UCS—Workers' Control: The Real Defence Against Unemployment is Attack!* Nicholson: *UCS—An Open Letter.* Fleet: *Whatever Happened at UCS.* Also Murray:

    UCS: The Anatomy of Bankruptcy, Spokesman Books, N
ham, 1972.

16. In April 1971, before the UCS crisis revealed itself, there we
30,000 unemployed men in Glasgow, a rise of 40% in one year.

17. In *The New Unionism*, op. cit.

18. A careful study of the state of trade union democracy in Britain
was made by John Hughes for the Royal Commission on Trade
Unions and Employers' Associations which worked under the
chairmanship of the late Lord Donovan. It was published as an
occasional paper by the Commission. Cf. Also Richard Fletcher:
Problems of Trade Union Democracy, IWC, 1971.

19. Cf. *The New Unionism*, Chapters on workers' control.

20. UCS: *The Social Audit*, A special report by the IWC, 1971.

21. The analysis of all such myths needs to begin with a study of the
first chapter of Karl Marx' *Capital*, in which he discusses the
nature of commodity-fetishism.

22. Hugh Scanlon, ibid.

3

ion as a Life-long Experience

What is the relationship between education and industry? This is a crucial question, but it is quite commonly avoided by educationalists, and particularly by educational reformers. Whenever we do meet it, it is usually to find that those asking it have subtly transformed it in order to assume an answer which is not too discomfiting either to the teaching profession or to industrialists. Of course, the question 'what does industry need from education?' poses quite a different set of problems to those we need to discuss. 'How can education better serve industry?' is the sort of conundrum that arises with every new phase of technological development: more schools, more colleges and universities must be opened to provide more scientists, more administrators, and more technically qualified workpeople, we are told at intervals of about a generation. The priorities in such questions are upside down and back to front. To see things the right way up, and to begin the pursuit of *education*, we must ask 'what sort of factories do our schools need?'

In the abstract, taking formal schooling at its best, there are few teachers who will not, when pushed, lay claim to the fundamental liberal commitment that their role is to stimulate the fullest possible development of their charges. The school, they feel, is properly an incubator of the free personality. That is to say, teachers commonly assume, or to be more accurate, think they assume, that they should treat their students each as an end in himself, and never as a mere means to serve some greater goal: whether that goal be the imagined good of the State, or the anticipated productivity of the Economy, or even, in these agnostic days, the alleged purpose of the Almighty. The old Jesuit boast that given care of a child until he reached the age of seven, he would be kept forever in the faith, is seen by the dominant educational consensus of today as almost the very epitome of evil. True, there are some who would explicitly repudiate liberal pretentions, but there are numerous good liberal swearwords to describe the results of such apostasy. 'Indoctrination', 'manipulation', 'brain-washing', 'propagandising' all spring to mind.

To remain on an equally abstract plane, there is not a factory, an office, a mine or a depot in the land in which these basic liberal assumptions can hold sway for a fraction of a moment, not even on Christmas Day when everyone is on holiday. No employer can treat his employees as ends in themselves, whose free personal development is the prime object of his enterprise. Indeed, no employer, however powerful, can easily imagine being so treated himself, even though it is his will, or the will of the élite grouping of which he forms a part, which has determined, often in precise detail, the major life options which are open to, or closed from, his subordinates. Few employers today actually *tell* their workmen that they are paid to work, not to think: but none are able to predicate their activities on any assumption other than that the goals and strategies of the enterprise, insofar as they are determined by anyone at all, must be rigidly monopolised by its directorate. Throughout the majority of modern industry, it is fair to be far more precise than this: individual initiative by an employee is commonly seen as at best an embarrassment, at worst a disruption, while the personal development of employees is considered a matter for their own pursuit, as best they can arrange it, in those parts of their lives which are called

C

'leisure'. Industry still seeks square pegs for square holes, and round pegs for round holes. Even in the comparatively rare cases where jobs are 'enlarged', or rotated, the modern division of labour remains, for the overwhelming majority of people, an absolute barrier to the development of their productive, or creative, capacities in any field other than the narrow strip to which they have been allotted. Proficiencies which can be learnt in days or weeks frequently become life-expectations. Such horizons can only tend to reduce people, unless they find ways to rebel against them.

The brutalising of work tends to turn leisure into passivity, or into an aggressively private activity: the alienated antithesis of compulsory labour. Modern industry, modern capitalism, far from constituting a celebration of the freedom of the individual, in fact represents a most systematic and extended denial of the basic conditions of that freedom.

But these are abstract statements, statements moreover of tendency, and they represent only part of the truth. The complex reality is that conditions of unfreedom repeatedly stimulate moods of rejection. Good schools reinforce this rejection, which will only hold out new hopes of fulfilment when subjection no longer remains the rule.

It remains true that the liberal educational goals are, at root, in flagrant contradiction to the basic assumptions which regulate our economic life. The result is that today, far from education—individual development in co-operative activity—reaching out through working life to become a life-long experience, it is still true that industry constantly exerts itself to reach its clammy hands down into the schools, in order to make wage-slavery as life-long, and as inescapable, as it possibly can. Of course, there are gross difficulties in the process. Although it is true that there are still all too many infant schools in which five-year-olds are aligned in ranks in wet play-

grounds and whistled into assembly, a ritual which
only meaningful as house-training for the factory and the
clocking-in queue, yet it remains quite undeniable that
modern pedagogy (which is the more necessary to industry as it desperately roots round to find expanded off-
square pegs to fit the new precision-made eccentric holes
of modern technology) is persistently rolling back the
age at which authoritarian discipline can be introduced.
Opening the 1972 Conference of the British National
Union of Teachers, the President of the organisation
claimed that in recent years there had been 'a new spirit
in the schools. The primary school today' he said, 'is a
place of adventure, experiment, liveliness, joy, and a
felicitous co-operation between child, parent and teacher.'

Such progress notwithstanding, and there is still room
for a great deal more of it, the school still serves its
masters. The more co-operative and participatory that
teaching techniques become, the more grossly they will
be out of phase with the roles for which their victims are
being prepared. The raising of the school leaving age
may see a rise in the age of secondary school mutiny:
but mutiny remains as likely as ever to nullify even the
best pedagogic intentions as the transition from class-
room to workshop becomes imminent. In the best imaginable case, if the schools were to succeed in wholly dedi-
cating themselves to the stimulation and liberation of
imagination throughout the whole school-life of their
pupils, then those pupils would be powerfully tempted to
drop out of the society into which they were subsequently
evicted. There are reformers, like Paul Goodman, who
welcome this prospect. To me it seems an unlikely bless-
ing. Denied access to any satisfactory outlet for productive effort, and denied facilities for creative communication unless they show exceptional talents, such rebels
are likely to develop into shallow hedonists, whose lives
will be prone to sterile introversion and dependency. If

a life-style, it is scarcely a *human* life-style:
...ld well have been arrested with the emerg-
...ommon cat, or for all we know, the garden
...ample possibilities for self-satisfaction at
...s sad level of expectation. If it were possible for schools
to ignore industry during the whole period of compulsory
education, and it is not, it would still be ethically impermissible for them to tolerate a factory system which
would give their pupils the choice of forgetting the most
important things they had learnt, or lapsing into social
parasitism. In fact, up to now, this discussion implies, if
anything, far too rosy a picture of the state of school
autonomy from the industrial power-complex. The whole
system of public examinations has no imaginable educational function, but is indispensible to the Labour Exchange. Tests of certain kinds can help both teachers and
students: but they help best when the student understands
that perhaps their most crucial function is to help the
teacher overcome his own inadequacies. There never was
a mark awarded that said anything incontrovertible about
the ability of a student, because 'ability' is a term which
includes a vast area of potential which can never be
measured until after it has been realised, and which can
(and should) remain open throughout a lifetime: but
every mark ever given does say something quite final
about the level of actual communication that has taken
place between a teacher and his charge. 'Bring out number, weight and measure' said Blake 'in a year of dearth'.
The mania for evaluation of students' performance would
be a healthy event, if it were a self-critical pedagogic
device. As it is, it tends to present a recurrent libel on
the capacities of those 'evaluated', which has the effect,
all too often, of self-fulfilling prophecy, convincing its
victims that *they* suffer from incapacities which are not
in truth their own, but their institutions'. Of course, if an
employer wants a French-speaking secretary, he has to

know that she can in fact speak French before he can employ her. Exams will be with us for a while yet: but we should know for what they were spawned, and refuse them the dignity of an *educational* rationale. Yet, in a negative way, they show us what vast developments are possible, by revealing some fraction of the *needs* which our current school system can never begin to meet. It is precisely when we are confronted by the results of measurements of 'performance' that we become aware of the pervasive influence of social status on the school structure. Poor kids do badly, rich kids do well. As J. W. B. Douglas reports in *The Home and the School:*

> 'When housing conditions are unsatisfactory, children make relatively low scores in the tests. This is so in each social class, but whereas middle-class children, as they get older, reduce this handicap, the manual working-class children from unsatisfactory homes fall even further behind; for them, overcrowding and other deficiencies at home have a progressive and depressive influence on their test performance.'

Bad housing is important as an indicator of this phenomenon, but its real root is occupational. Unskilled workers are badly paid, which is why they live on poor estates or in slums. Slum housing is certainly a handicap, but it is not an insuperable handicap on its own. Half-blind Sean O'Casey saw more colour in the world from a Dublin tenement than most duchesses can find in a room full of Titians. Abraham Lincoln was reportedly conceived in a log cabin, but his step-mother taught him to read the Bible, *Pilgrim's Progress*, and *Robinson Crusoe*. You have to apply other clamps to the imagination than poor housing if you are to achieve any success in the effort to paralyse it. In British slums, the majority of fathers and mothers have never been introduced to Bunyan or Defoe, or for that matter to any other major writer in our language, so it is hardly surprising if their children read late, and with difficulty. For years it was fashionable to consider this fact as the outcome of genetic determination. The unskilled were not culturally deprived because they were poor and unskilled, but because they were born that way. This was not the view of the classic theorists of industrialism. Adam Smith, who began his greatest work with the celebration of the productive merits of the division of labour, was well aware of its baneful influence on the labourer. His insights on this matter were enlarged in different ways by Owen, Ruskin, and Marx, to say nothing of the whole pleiad of romantic novelists, poets, and publicists. What is perfectly clear is that as factories stabilised themselves as the predominant form of productive unit through society, so the divergence of talents was widened, and transmitted across generations. The industrial division of labour became the solid foundation of an industrial class system. For all its onesidedness, there are few descriptions of this process which are more compelling and more farsighted than that of de Tocqueville, in *Democracy in America:*

'When a workman is unceasingly and exclusively engaged in the fabrication of one thing, he ultimately does his work with singular dexterity; but at the same time he loses the general faculty of applying his mind to the direction of the work. He every day becomes more adroit and less industrious; so that it may be said of him that in proportion as the workman is improved the man is degraded . . . When a workman has spent a considerable portion of his existence in this manner, his thoughts are for ever set upon the object of his daily toil; his body has contracted certain fixed habits, which it can never shake off: in a word, he no longer belongs to himself, but to the calling which he has chosen. It is in vain that laws and manners have been at pains to level all barriers around such a man, and to open to him on every side a thousand different paths to fortune: a theory of manufactures more powerful than manners and laws binds him to a craft, and frequently to a spot, which he cannot leave: it assigns him a certain place in society beyond which he cannot go: in the midst of universal movement it has rendered him stationary.

'In proportion as the principle of the division of labour is more extensively applied, the workman becomes more weak, more narrow-minded, and more dependent. The art advances, the artisan recedes . . .'

This savage prophecy has not been by any means fulfilled in full, for two good reasons. First, for the reason that people *will* resist de-humanisation, however high the cost of resistance, and however long the odds against their success. The whole story of trade unionism, and the entire vicarious history of the socialist movement, bear witness to this fact. As a result of it, the basic liberal humanist ideals survive the process which de Tocqueville traced, which is, of course, at one level, itself the result of the operation of the liberal doctrine in economic life. Secondly, the prophecy fails because the story of the development of industrial capitalism is an account of the unleashing of a succession of technological upheavals, during which the division of labour is recurrently recast. On one side this results from time to time in the demand for new skills and higher educational levels: but at the same time, on the other side it repeatedly gives rise to the displacement of old skills and the social rejection of all those people whose inflexibility (whether because they are old, or because they have been inadequately taught in their youth) keeps them below the threshold of profitable employment. So-called technological unemployment is not a new phenomenon, although in its recent forms it has the capacity to create wider unease in the body politic than heretofore. Its true source is not abstract technology, which, being inanimate, is socially neutral, but specific technologies in the service of capital, whose dominance depends upon the control of equipment and processes, and upon the subordination of the interests of people to the imperatives of its balance-sheets.

Adam Smith had adumbrated three component benefits of the division of labour: it augmented productivity by specialisation, increasing the proficiency of workmen by intensifying their dexterity; it saved time by cutting out transfers between operations; and it facilitated the introduction and development of machines. To these three principles, Charles Babbage, in *The Economy of Manufactures*, added a fourth:

> 'That the master manufacturer, by dividing the work to be executed into different processes, each requiring different degrees of skill and force, can purchase exactly that precise quantity of both of which is necessary for each process.'

With this perception rose the possibility of the whole school of scientific management, as subsequently developed by F. W. Taylor in the United States. The more intensively processes could be controlled, the more dependent roles were created for employees, and the less the industrial currency of the liberal ideal of an integrated human personality. Babbage recorded the process in 1832 without noticing the implication of his words:

> '. . . if the whole work were to be executed by one workman, that person must possess sufficient skill to perform the most difficult, and sufficient strength to execute the most laborious, of the operations into which the art is divided.'

Just about fifty years were to elapse before Taylor was

to refine this insight to the point where he could insist, without shame, that:

'One of the very first requirements for a man who is fit to handle pig iron as a regular occupation is that he shall be so stupid and so phlegmatic that he more nearly resembles an ox than any other type.'

The logical result of such specialisation was clearly expressed in the dire anti-utopia of H. G. Wells' *The Time Machine*, in which exploration of the future revealed that effete aristocrats and feelingless plebians had evolved into two distinct and incompatible species. If the logical result is not to be anticipated in the actual outcome, we owe the fact both to human resilience and to the contradictory implications of advancing techniques. While Taylorism in its classic prescriptions gained a considerable following, in spite of protests, in the mass production industries of the Ford school, subsequent work methods have evolved alongside electronic techniques to produce quite different notions of job control. Nevertheless, Taylorism was an innovatory discipline which cast a long shadow before it, and even today, in the discussion of job-enlargement, rotation of tasks, 'participatory' reform, and kindred expedients, the ghost of scientific management can still be heard speaking, in a variety of accents it is true, but with no diminution of its anti-human intent. It is the same ghost which speaks in the debate on educational methods and reform of the schools. 'More means worse', it says. Selection and specialisation are its necessary watchwords. Its cardinal principle it transfers from Babbage's factories to the secondary modern schools and the lower streams of the alleged comprehensives which spring up on all sides. 'Spend no more than is necessary on human formation' it whispers. Surplus of training is dysfunctional: overeducated operatives are indisciplined and refractory. In a square hole, square people are opti-

mal, and tendencies to deviate into roundness must be
rigidly clamped out.

Yet all the time, industry needs education. A modest
explosion has recently taken place in certain forms of
continuation courses, in adult classes of a particular kind,
in shop steward training, and in technical education,
since the passage in Britain of the Industrial Training
Act, which levies a toll on firms in order to ensure that
if they do not train their own workers, they will be
forced to pay to train other people's. A much bigger
convulsion is called for, but is unlikely to take place. But
all this effort, and most of the proposed effort which will
not be undertaken, is conceived within the essential
framework of the constricting assumptions we have been
discussing. We *could* have a real transformation in education *at* work, but the price would not be simply the
universalisation of day-release courses, desirable though
that may be. A genuine transformation would involve
education *in* work, self-education, community education,
in the generation of real moves towards collective self-
management of industry. Only such a revolution would
abolish the stultifying role-patterns which are imposed
on work-people, and only such a revolution would open
up the possibility, and the need, for every man to seek
the continuous enlargement of his powers and his basic
knowledge of the world in which he was working.

Universalist education is incompatible with the rigid
division of labour which forms men into porters and
philosophers, and aligns them into opposing social classes.
Both in work, and in whatever preparation which en-
lightened people come to agree it may be necessary to
make for work, the division of labour as we understand
it is more than a net disincentive to free personal development. Within it, 'equality of opportunity' comes to
mean the will o' the wisp of an equal start in a fundamentally unequal race: and all the nobility of the watch-

word is transformed into sleazy apologetics. Free development of each personality to its outer limits means the systematic encouragement and fostering of talents, and this will never begin until factories begin to be schools, and self-governing schools at that. Only then will schools cease to be factories for the engineering of human beings into employees. Perhaps a hundred years ago, this was a utopian message. Today, it is direly practical: the only resource which we possess in virtual abundance is that of human potential, and yet it is that resource which we squander with even greater profligacy than we eat up the earth's finite material resources. Mankind will soon need all the wits and creativity which it is stifling every day in modern industry, and its appendage, modern education, if it is to find the way to live out another century.

First published in 1973

4

A Lesson from Belgium

The Belgian trade unions, which organise almost two million members, are among the strongest, proportionally speaking, in Europe, and constitute a major social force in their own country. 66.95% of the eligible workpeople in Belgium are enrolled in their unions: the result is that these organisations are able to play a major part in the political life of the country, and between them, sustain well over 100 members of Parliament. The shortrun political influence of the trade union movement is, rather strangely, actually increased by the fact that two major federations exist: one aligned with the Socialist Party, and the other with the Catholic Christian Social Party. What must certainly constitute a source of weakness in many struggles has at the same time the paradoxical effect of exposing the Catholic Party to internal pressure from its allied trade unions, a pressure from which it cannot escape in the same way as it most certainly would, if all unions were affiliated to the rival socialist party.[1] Doubtless, this fact plays its own part in incorporating Belgian workers into the political structures which they have inherited: but for this, authority must pay a certain price in sensitivity to the corporate interests of Labour.

In 1965, membership of the various central union federations was as follows:

Confederation of Christian Unions (CSC)	844,410
Belgian General Federation of Labour (FGTB)	734,805

General Central Association of Liberal
          Trade Unions (CGSLB)   122,299
Central Association of Unified Unions   42,500
Independent Union's Centre   58,000
Total   1,802,034

The two major federations are associated with the major political[2] parties. Most of the 'Liberal' unionists (for which in current English terms, 'conservative' might be a better rubric) are recruited from professional strata. The reasons for the numerical preponderance of the Catholic Unions have more to do with the development of the Belgian economy than with any primarily ideological commitment: each union centre has always drawn its main strength from certain areas of the country, and the power base of the Socialist FGTB has been in the declining French-speaking Walloon provinces, hard hit by the retrenchments in the coal and steel industries; while the growth sector of the economy has been in the predominantly Catholic Flemish-speaking coastal provinces, in which three-quarters of the members of the CSC are to be found. But Christian trade unionism has not come to the front in Belgium by means of simple inertia and sectarian commitment: it has in fact benefited from the rise of new social attitudes in the Church, and it has attracted a substantial cadre of active and capable organisers. The greater membership of the CSC is more dispersed than that of the FGTB, which is concentrated into a number of large-scale industries. Twelve industrial centres are affiliated to the FGTB: fourteen to the CSC. The Catholic unions recruit widely in textiles, food, and chemicals. In the FGTB, the three major organisations of engineering workers, public service employees, and general workers account between them for 67% of the total membership.[3]

The background to the development of industry in

Belgium cannot be understood without understanding the strange game of leapfrog which has gone on between Wallonia and Flanders since the constitution of the Belgian national state.

The first industrial revolution was, in Belgium, concentrated in Wallonia. From the second half of the eighteenth century, wool, coal, linen and cotton industries began to develop in the modern sense. Individual entrepreneurs gave place to joint-stock companies between 1825 and 1835, under the stimulus of the first major bank in the country, *La Société Générale*. As Ernest Mandel has pointed out, this was

'From the beginning a mixed bank, that is both a deposit and an investment bank, owning important holdings in innumerable industrial, financial, commercial and transport concerns. Belgium is thus the birth-place of finance capital in the Marxist sense: banking capital which flows into industry, substitutes shares for credit, and exercises close control over company management. Belgian finance capital acquired a dominant position in the economy of the country half a century before the same phenomenon occurred in Germany, France, U.S.A., Italy and elsewhere.'[4]

As Mandel comments, it is not at all surprising that Belgium became in turn, the first mainland European country to start building railways; the owner of the densest rail-network in the world; the pioneer of railway-building abroad as far afield as Russia, Egypt, Mexico and China; a prodigious exporter of capital and techniques, and the proprietor of a Royal Colony, the Congo, administered by the *Société Générale*. Up to 1914 the opulence of the Belgian middle-classes was unrivalled, as was the squalor of the workers. The Catholic culture was reinforced by the fact that the Church dominion over

education was only breached with difficulty during a pro-
tracted struggle with the Liberal Party: throughout this
struggle the political structure was jealously controlled
by the upper and middle classes, organised into Catholic
and Liberal Parties. The working-class battle for the suffrage was particularly long drawn-out and hard. After a
General Strike in 1893 the right to vote was gained by
male workers, but this operated within the framework of
a plural voting system which seriously handicapped the
working-class electors. The Catholic Party began to form
its trade unions only when the battle for equal male suffrage was about to be conceded, as it was, in the end,
after the First World War. But once the decision had
been taken, the Catholic Church put out a formidable
range of co-operative and social organisations which,
linked with the new unions, and concentrated in the still
largely rural provinces, provided, for new industrialists,
a much needed alternative to the militant socialist unions
which had come to dominate the already industrialised
French-speaking provinces. The enhanced stability of
labour relations in Flanders brought in its turn further
industrial development.

Mandel has documented the close interplay between
class and region in Belgian political life. In a nutshell,
Flanders remained not only economically, but also politically subordinate until the early thirties. A national resurgence of Flemings, part-socialist, part-fascist, supported by some of the lesser clergy, but opposed by the
Catholic hierarchy (as in the national struggle in Ireland)
finally gained equal linguistic rights in 1932. From this
time onwards, the majority party in Belgium was 'naturally' Catholic and indeed, constantly augmented by
the higher Northern birthrate. Of course, catholics could
be persuaded to vote outside confessional lines, but until
they did, either straying to support the fascists or the
socialists, their party was in permanent ascendency. The

Catholic Party itself adroitly accomplished the transition
from arch-reactionary spokesmen of the needs of doctrine
and the interests of a narrow upper stratum, to broadly-
based middle-class party with cross-class support. Fundamentally the Flemish ascendency continued until the
early nineteen-sixties, when the economic decline of
Wallonia precipitated the sudden rise of trade union supported Walloon nationalism, which profoundly affected
the political life of the nation.

In this context grew the socialist trade unions. The
Belgian Labour Party was formed in 1885, and advocated
a socialist programme from the beginning. A federation
of trade union, co-operative and political bodies, it gave
great stimulus to the formation of new co-operative and
mutual aid societies, and as it grew, so did union membership. Trade unionism was radicalised by the extreme
reluctance of the Belgian ruling class to yield political
rights to the working people: in addition to the General
Strike of 1893, the Party called similar strikes in 1902
and 1912 for the democratisation of the suffrage. It
was during this period that Rosa Luxemburg said that
European workers should 'learn to speak Belgian'. She
was demanding the supple combination of direct action
and parliamentary politics which evolved during the
battle for an equal franchise. Once the male suffrage had
been conceded on a basis of equality, in 1919, the socialists increased their parliamentary representation from 34
to 70, receiving more than 36% of the votes cast. This
victory cost the still predominantly reactionary Catholic
Party the majority it had held since 1884. A Catholic-
Socialist coalition ensued, and this produced notable
social legislation, including the eight-hour day and a law
permitting peaceful picketing in strikes. This coalition
broke up when the socialists opted for opposition, and
with a brief exception, they remained in opposition until
the middle-thirties. The received structure had clearly

settled to produce a permanent division at something near to parity, and it was only when the national movement in Flanders formally divided into socialist and fascist wings that the balance was disturbed to the point that Labour could win the largest number of Parliamentary seats. During this time Henri De Man developed his particular politics of 'revisionism' aimed at the conquest of middle-class support, while a powerful left-wing socialist current, headed by Paul-Henri Spaak, developed to the point at which its leader could enter the Cabinet and change his opinions. The political impasse continued with socialists in office, since no fundamental structural change was possible within the rules of the elaborate parliamentary game which had evolved. Socialist ministers reigned and equivocated while strikes on popular front scale spread out from France and erupted through the country, and the inevitable disillusionment which followed cost them their temporary political lead, before the Nazi invasion.

The invasion drove some socialist leaders into exile, while De Man remained behind and advocated the dissolution of the Labour Party, whose members, he advocated, should 'enter the cadres of national resurrection'.[5] Other more numerous activists chose the alternative course of resistance and sabotage, and this experience produced a radicalisation of the union militants, and a split in the Socialist federation, the then CGT. At the end of the Second World War, the International Federation of Trade Unions sent a delegation to Brussels, Ghent, Liege and Antwerp and convened a representative conference in Brussels. They found four separate fractions among the unions: the old CGT leaders, the left-wing socialist breakaway CGT, the Communists and the Catholics. The IFTU spokesmen pushed for unification, and although they failed to bring the Catholics into a common federation, in 1945 the two wings of the socialist move-

ment reunited. By September that year the new FGTB
had won half a million members.[6] The FGTB gained its
unity at the price of its integral membership of the socialist party, and from then on normally occupied a place to
the left of the Party in the political spectrum, whereas,
before the war, the union had traditionally been largely
to the right of the party. As Mandel has reported:

> 'The left wing was moulded by the strong personality
> of André Renard. This dynamic leader of the metal
> workers of Liege had retained from his youth strong
> anarcho-syndicalist sympathies, and had little confi-
> dence in classic reformist policies, whether in Parlia-
> ment or in wage negotiations with employers . . . he
> was able to forge the Liege unions into an extremely
> powerful weapon. On four separate occasions in 1946,
> in 1948, in 1950 and in 1957, the strikes which he led
> at Liege wrested important concessions from employers
> and from succeeding Governments, including govern-
> ments with socialist participation'.[7]

Renard was the pioneer of the policy of 'Structural
Reforms', which figured in the programme he presented
in 1954 and again in 1956 at the FGTB Congresses.

'Structural Reform' is a slogan which has been inter-
preted in contradictory ways. In the hands of the Italian
Communist Party it has meant little more than a policy
of nationalisation and reforming legislation, with few
significant differences from the sense of, say, the reform programme of the 1945 Labour Government in
Britain. But in the strategy of the FGTB, 'structural reform' is at once a policy of mobilisation for change at
the grass roots, and a series of coherent and specific
demands on the legislature. It is therefore a realistic
and genuinely radical programme since it is able, at
the same time, to arouse the necessary social movement for socialist change and to pose the practical tests

which any such radical movement must be able to apply
to any body of its representatives. In this way, the Belgian
trade unions had moved beyond the constricting formula
of 'a minimum programme' of immediate reforms (higher
pensions, more public housing, even some nationalisation) all bearing the scantest imaginable relationship
to the ultimate goal of the socialist movement, which
involves the libertarian transformation of all social re-
lationships. The FGTB had reached a programmatic solution to an age-old problem for socialists everywhere, to
wit, how to link their immediate demands with their
dreams of the new society. The proposals contained a
transitional element capable of arousing appetites and
widening aspirations for change to the most audacious
degree, yet always practical and down-to-earth. It was
thus possible to envisage the overcoming of the inherent
problem of socialists: that in the capitalist countries,
socialists are divided into practical men who aim to
change nothing substantial in society, and idealistic
dreamers, who possess the *will* for change but wield none
of the effective power to bring it about.

At the time that the FGTB embraced the cause of
structural reform, the Socialist Party was engaged in an
alliance with the Liberals, aimed at eroding Catholic influence by eating away public subsidies to Catholic
schools.[8] The price of coalition with the Liberals was a
freeze on all kinds of even mildly reforming actions, and
had the FGTB accepted the strategy, they would have
been outflanked on their left by the Catholic Unions
which in the circumstances could afford quite militant
policies. The strategy was bound to be self-defeating on
the electoral plane since it could only promote Catholic
solidarity. But the fact that the FGTB rallied around an
alternative programme produced a struggle within the
Socialist Party in which the union-led caucus won a
formal victory in 1958. At this point, the ambiguity in

the structural reform programme became clear: after a verbal surrender, the socialist leaders evolved their own kind of 'structural' change involving no more than the kind of industrial rationalisation and indicative planning that became familiar, later, in Mr. Wilson's Britain. The Belgians were beguiled with all the rhetoric of incomes policy, and suffered many of the onslaughts of 'redeployment' before these wolves in sheeps' clothing were set loose in the British Labour Movement. In 1960 a great strike broke out over the introduction, by the Catholic Eyskens Government, of a *loi unique* aimed at restoring an ailing economy at the expense of the working population. This General Strike brought about the defeat of the Eyskens Administration, and the General Election which followed produced, yet again, another coalition. But in spite of the rhetoric of the socialist political leaders, no anti-capitalist structural reforms were forthcoming from this Government, no actions were taken against the holding companies in favour of extending trade union rights, and in the crisis of morale which afflicted the socialist ranks as a result the renewed upsurge of Walloon nationalism produced sharp conflicts and splits.[9]

All of this could only reinforce the lesson, that the anti-capitalist content of structural reforms must be made abundantly plain, and the emphasis on workers' control as a key element in socialist strategy must be completely clear, if sufficient forces are ever to be assembled to insist upon the beginning of the transition to socialism. And it is this lesson which served to revive and intensify the keen discussion on workers' control within the FGTB.

The resultant programme remains a reform programme, whilst continuing the spirit of contestation and struggle. In it, the unions pin-point the vital need to maintain their autonomy of action, their initiative and their right to oppose. To this extent, the FGTB advances a genuine workers' control strategy, and not a policy of subordinate 'participation'. Naturally, all who see the struggle for economic democracy as an unremitting process, based upon the developing understanding of wider and wider sections of the working populace, confront the same dilemmas which are faced by the Belgian unions.

As their programme says:

'For the FGTB, participation necessarily implies the maintenance of union autonomy. It is in this context that we can describe workers' control in the following manner:

1. *Who?*
The FGTB considers that workers' control cannot be effected except by the workers organised into unions. Solidarity and cohesion amongst the workers in their unions is the guarantee of the defence of their interests: isolated workers cannot enjoy such benefits.

2. *When?*
The essential conditions for workers' control are that they should be informed in time, that is, that they should be informed previous to any decisions being taken and never be faced with a fait accompli.

3. *Of What?*
Of all the factors in any given economic and social situation. Thus it is not a matter of information limited to a few texts or other items, but on the contrary, the sum of elements must be presented to allow a rounded judgement of the situation.

4. *Why?*
So that there is the possibility (not the obligation) of exercising the right of dispute, that is to say, of presenting, if need be, our own alternative proposals. It is important to insist on the word 'possibility'; this means

that the union reserves for itself the right to choose the time, the conditions, the duration and the issues with regard to which it might decide, completely autonomously, to exercise its right of dispute.

5. *On What Levels?*
Workers' control must be exercised at all levels (enterprise, groups of enterprises, region, industrial sector, nation . . .) in close association with all the workers concerned.

6. *How is union freedom to be safeguarded?*
The union must at the same time safeguard its entire freedom of industrial action, its entire autonomy. The right of dispute does not only consist in safeguarding union autonomy, but also in promoting settlements which render this freedom of union activity technically possible.

Workers' control consists of continual limitation of arbitrary action on the part of the employers, thanks to measures permitting the intervention of the workers in areas which, previously, escaped them—by progressive conquests within the framework of the unions which preserve the autonomy of their rights and powers, which are continuously being renewed, assuring for the workers progressive mastery over economic and social life at all levels.

In a certain number of cases, management decisions concerning investment, for example, risk limiting the real margins for workers' claims. It is therefore essential for the unions to be able to advocate a settlement which re-establishes this margin for social progress.'[10]

It is always possible for groups, even large organisations, of workpeople to bargain for greater powers and then discover themselves wielding responsibilities which are larger than those powers warrant. 'Incorporation' is a constant snare. Yet advance cannot be made without running risks, and these risks can only be minimised if the unions remain open to correction by their members, and sensitive to the complex problems involved in retaining the capacity for autonomous action. In a word, workers must control their unions before they can wrest even minimal advances in control over their work. But more: as the Belgian strategy makes plain, the unions need to operate on the level of the economy as well as that of the factory, and therefore require an effective political arm. So workers must control their parties before they can advance to control their economies. None of this is easy. And all the time, the employers and their political spokesmen can maintain cohesive organisations which have great flexibility and manipulate opinion through most of the modern brain-washing media.

Yet there is no alternative to this struggle other than surrender of all hopes for equality, all dreams of freedom. If workers prove incapable of controlling their own organisations, they remain manifestly unable to reach further afield. To the extent that their appetite for freedom is awakened, they can see the need for effective organisation to reach it. Of course, there is no guarantee that authority will allow a peaceful revolution to consolidate itself peacefully: but equally, there is not the slightest chance that the people will awaken in a violent revolution unless they are thwarted in the attempt to make a non-violent one. So that whether modern socialists place themselves in the 'physical force' or the 'moral force' camps of the industrial Charter, they cannot afford to by-pass the questions posed to them by the Belgian Trade Unions. In fact, as always, the working-class movement will, in Mao Tse-Tung's words, need to 'walk on two legs'. It will need direct action, on an ascending scale. It will need 'constitutional' reform, parliamentary enactment, on an ascending scale. It will need, to secure this combination of measures, the vision to define its goals and its strategy with the utmost clarity, and the will to unite to pursue them. In short, to re-echo Rosa Luxemburg, it will need to 'learn to speak Belgian' yet again, if socialism is ever to become a viable option in late-capitalist Europe.

FOOTNOTES

1. For a discussion of this process, see *European Political Parties:* P.E.P. Allen & Unwin, 1969, p.76 et seq.
2. Cf. Stephen Holt: *Six European States.* Hamish Hamilton, 1970, p.290.
3. Cf. Walter Kendall: Trade Unions in Belgium and Luxemburg, *European Community* 8-9, 1970, p.21 et seq.
4. Ernest Mandel: The Dialectic of Class and Region in Belgium. *New Left Review.* 20, p.6.
5. H. W. Laidler: *History of Socialism.* Routledge & Kegan Paul, 1968, p.494 et seq.
6. *Forty-Five Years—IFTU*, by Walter Schevenels. IFTU 1956.
7. Op. cit., p.21.
8. Op. cit.
9. Cf. Marcel Deneckere: How Can the Left Come to Power in Belgium? *International Socialist Journal*, no. 5-6, p.586 et seq.
10. Cf. *A Trade Union Strategy in the Common Market*, Spokesman Books, 1971.

Democracy and the Environment

Somewhat belatedly, the socialist movement has begun to face up to some of the issues which are involved in the increasingly urgent debate on the environment. In Britain, the argument has broken out across the whole spectrum of the left, involving Wayland Young in the Fabian Society, C.A.R. Crosland from the front bench of the Parliamentary Labour Party, John Lewis and the readers of the Communist Party's newspaper the *Morning Star,* and some few voices of the New Left. Crosland has sprung to the defence of working-class standards of life, to urge that trade unionists have a right to take their holidays in Majorca even if (as he implies in a characteristically snobbish aside) this implies the proliferation of fish and chip shops in that once blessed haven.[1] Trade unionists might well have been grateful for this advocacy during the days in which Crosland's own administration was busily restricting their purchasing power in the interests of the defence of sterling: but they will need stronger defences than Crosland's new-found 'populism' if they are to resist the new onslaught that will fall on them, which will undoubtedly seek legitimacy in the appeal to environmental conservation.

Of course, there *is* an ecological crisis. Its precise boundaries and significance remain to some extent open to argument, since there may well be some case for caution in the extrapolation of existing trends over a prolonged time-scale. As Professor Kapp has pointed out, a computer set to work in 1872 would have predicted that

the density of horse-drawn traffic would by now be so
great as to render all our cities impassable: choked as
they would be with an impenetrable deposit of horse-
dung.[2] The new technologies have been developing with
remarkable speed, and much of the discussion of their
likely effect is bound to be to some degree conjectural,
not only until their side effects and other implications
have had some time to manifest themselves, but also their
longevity can be assessed, and their degree of liability to
supercession by still further new technologies estimated.
Yet it is impossible to dismiss as simply misplaced certain of the central arguments of what has become the
ecology lobby: while this movement contains its own
bizarre and reactionary voices, and while it frequently
betrays a lack of sociological sophistication, it has nonetheless produced a volume of hard evidence which already
demands not only scrutiny, but also action.

More than a century ago, Marx repeatedly warned
against the fact that 'all progress in capitalistic agriculture
is a progress in the art, not only of robbing the labourer,
but of robbing the soil; all progress in increasing the
fertility of the soil for a given time, is a progress towards
ruining the lasting sources of that fertility. The more a
country starts its development on the foundation of
modern industry, like the United States, for example, the
more rapid is this process of destruction. Capitalist production, therefore, develops technology, and the combin-
ing together of various processes into a social whole, only
by sapping the original sources of all wealth—the soil
and the labourer.'[3] The works of the Ehrlichs, Com-
moners, Meadows and others, whatever other effects they
may have, assuredly serve to provide at any rate a partial
documentation of the results of the evolution, over a
hundred years of blind rapacity, of capitalism's extraordinary 'success'.

Traditional socialism has in its theoretical arsenal two

responses to this state of affairs. The first of these concerns the critique of the market economy, which, for a by no means negligible part of the ecological lobby, seems, however inconsistently, to remain a basic presumption, a sacred cow. Labour movements will soon discover this truth, because the administrators of the market economy, once alerted to the environmental problems their institutions have created, will spare no efforts to present the bill for them to the very work-people who are the main sufferers from the ill-effects both of the problems themselves and the institutions which have given rise to them. Socialists must therefore take the offensive, not merely to ensure that capitalism is presented with its own bills, but also to determine that it be forced into liquidation as soon as possible.

There is a second traditional socialist insight which is crucial to the consideration of this issue, if the whole argument is not to be allowed to become a pretext for a new conservative authoritarianism. This is linked with the first, but is by no means reducible to it: it concerns the basic assumption of Marx, which was that capitalism saps not only the productivity of the soil, but also that of the labourer. Of all the resources available to mankind, the only virtually infinite one is that of human potential. Before one can give a definitive answer to the question of how many human beings can survive in a given space with given materials, one has to know what kind of human beings are under consideration. Presumably there was an optimum population as well as a maximum population which was capable of survival in the environment confronting paleolithic men. Whatever specific figures might be put on these populations, they were vastly smaller than those which could apply to primitive agriculturalists, and these in turn were very much less than those relevant to civilisation, in the dawn of metal technology.

Man and his environment have always existed in reciprocal inter-action, and the same constellation of natural elements has been proved capable of bearing radically different meanings for men at different levels of intellectual development and technical prowess. There is every reason to believe that each technology has its frontiers of potential; but we shall never be able to delineate those frontiers fully until we have answered first the question of how far technologies themselves are contained and distorted within the restrictive presumptions of divided and exploitative societies. Other societies than modern capitalism have collapsed. None could be said to have fallen for want of technology in the abstract: indeed history is full of accounts of ruined civilisations which were structurally incapable of utilising and developing the techniques they had already begun to discover.

The Greeks made elaborate toys incorporating some of the basic principles of steam engines at Alexandria: but they had no need for mechanical motive force when there was adequate slave-power on call, so that their discoveries had a purely academic significance. The development of Ancient science has been shown to have repeatedly run into cul-de-sacs, not because of any want of abstract intellectual capacity, but because the social structures of Greece and Rome created life-styles and expectations among the leisured classes which militated against experimentalism and applied practical intellectual activity in many fields.[4] In war, or in Government, the inhibitions may have been less formidable than they were in husbandry, medicine, and the practical arts of economic production: even in war, however, the class structure exercised its pernicious enfeebling influence over time. To remain in this comparatively narrow field of enquiry, we would be bound to recognise that neither the Greek nor the Roman civilisations floundered because of their technological rigidity, but that they fell because of the contradictory pressures generated within their oppressive social structures, which exercised their own baleful influence on technological development.

Again and again throughout history we find instances of this same phenomenon. In the writings of Ibn Khaldun, the Arab scholar who founded historical sociology in the 14th Century, we find an account of the cycle of governmental styles in hydraulic society, as dynasty succeeds dynasty and replicates its trajectory, through the generations, from popular upsurge to oppressive tyranny, from restorer and custodian of the irrigation works to parasite, war lord and vainglorious builder of state monuments among the recurrent droughts and floods produced by the neglect of water conservation. The Ch'in dynasty in China had sufficient technology to consolidate the unification of the country by unifying its canals: it did not have adequate politics or social science to prevent the recurrent neglect and abuse of that technology, and recurrent cycle of 'good' and 'bad' government which was later to be noted by Ibn Khaldun in the somewhat different circumstances of the near East.

Even when advanced techniques have been imported neat from other cultures, class structures have frequently proved insufficiently plastic to utilise them. This is true even in the military domain, where opportunism is normally well-developed. A classic case is that of the introduction of firearms into the Mamluk kingdom: the development of the arquebus, general throughout Europe for more than a century before the final confrontation between the Mamluks and the Ottomans, was meaningless to a military caste which identified status with cavalry and could not delegate critical responsibility to mere foot-soldiers. Throughout crucial struggles the decisive weapons could only be wielded by slaves. The Mamluks were routed.[5]

Modern capitalism has liberated an explosion in technical capacities, and has created the preconditions for a global society. But it has no more solved the problem of class antagonism, of internecine social war, than did the Ancients with their slaves, or the oriental despots in the great river-based civilisations. Both inside the great capitalist metropoles, and outside them in the subordinated territories over which they hold sway, class struggles are a fundamental fact of life. That the ascendent class is today an entrepreneurial one only adds the burden of market domination to that of political subordination. In such a context, technology is *always* distorted. Social priorities emerge by a process of aggravated indetermination, to ensure that millions shall starve while inconceivable wealth is pledged to the task of lunar exploration. More ingenuity is lavished on research into the production of harmful detergents than on the investigation of cancer, while the goal of enabling a few men to traverse the Atlantic in three and a half hours assumes greater importance, and demands much greater investment, than that of enabling the majority of citizens in a small country like Britain to cross their own capital city in the same time.

In modern capitalist industry, which produces an increasing number of technical miracles which hardly anyone wants, the vast majority of human beings develop only a tiny fraction of their capacities. Large numbers of production processes exist which can pre-empt the waking hours of an enormous labour force, often for some transparently silly purpose, without stimulating in their victims anything other than the most basic mechanical skills and a developed capacity for alienated day-dreams. This artificial diminution of human beings is one of the major triumphs of capitalist industrial organisation, and must be considered as having some weight in any explanation for the astonishing longevity of the system. The process is never complete, and there are welcome signs that it is less and less able to function adequately, as technologies demand higher levels of skill in at least part of the labour-force, and as competition stimulates appetites which it cannot slake. Even so, the manifold deprivations inflicted upon the human victims of capitalism begin with, and culminate in, the restriction of their potential for self-development. Any ecology which ignores this fact ignores the fundamental problem, and can only be expected to develop into a form of elitist anti-humanism. The present significance of the movement for workers' control and socialist self-management is not that it already provides the answers to this problem, but only that it faces the question. Unless this question *is* faced, the only conceivable strategy for preserving the environment from the ruin which is predicted for it is a narrowly restrictive one, based on curbing the elementary appetites of the many, while quite possibly stimulating all the silliest and greediest fads against which ecologists rightly complain, in order to develop the 'proven' capacities of the few.

Does this mean that the Malthusian echoes which are to be heard on all sides lack all foundation in science? Hardly. Malthus remains as wrong as he ever was, but there *is* a population problem for capitalist-imperialist society, and it may well be 'solved' by the inhuman processes predicted by so many ecologists. If we say that developed people can make more of an unpromising environment than undeveloped people, this does not mean they can levitate themselves above all material problems. But the major material problem of the modern world remains that of its social structure, which generates a whole series of obstacles to the solution of all other material problems. First, it thwarts personal human growth and therefore the progress of art and science. Mute inglorious Miltons abound within it, because it mutes them. But secondly, thwarted people are more easily constrained to develop thwarted needs, to seek

surrogate satisfactions, and commonly, to compensate
for the frustration of their spiritual, intellectual needs by
the generation of quite peculiar material appetites. This
opens up the whole question of what is involved in the
concept of 'need', and to this we shall have to return.

Further, the same atavistic social arrangements commonly prevent the utilisation of any technology but the
most 'advanced', whose relative advancement may be, in
human terms, that is to say, in terms of its practical use-
fulness to a given people within a particular terrain,
highly questionable, but whose ascendancy is determined
by its market superiority. The weight of this deformation
of rational technique is felt above all in the undeveloped
countries, where it is joined by the weight of controlled
non-development of vital resources. To the extent that
the World Health Organisation makes improvements in
life-expectation, in the birth-rate, and in overcoming
child mortality, in these countries, while UNCTAD fails
to do anything at all to reverse the trade imbalance
which is constantly aggravating their adverse economic
position, medical technology merely intensifies the contradictions which have prevented the social order from
liberating any appropriate scientific response to the para-
mount needs of those territories. There is only one answer
which is realistic for such countries: it is revolution.
Revolution alone will tackle the economic development
crisis: and in the process it will not fail to tackle the
population problem, not for Malthusian reasons, but in
response to the demands of revolutionary women for
their own rights to develop as creative people.

In such revolution can be seen some key elements of
the solution to the wider environmental crisis. The fact
of uneven development, noticed so keenly by Lenin,
which produced the industry of Pittsburgh alongside the
plantations of Cambodia, and the living standards of
Detroit car-workers alongside those of Vietnamese rice-

growers, is paralleled by a strange form of combined development.

As American Armies took the field in Korea and Vietnam, resting on the hyper-developed technology of their extraordinarily powerful economic base, so they produced a reaction among their antagonists. The Vietnamese, whose economic development at the beginning of the conflict was as scant as is imaginable, found themselves confronting a colossus. In fighting it, they were compelled to develop a politico-military machine of equal complexity: a human collective which could match the most sophisticated computer hardware which was ranged against it. This extended and intricately co-ordinated division of political and military labour could never have evolved from the paddy-fields alone. It arose to meet a specific and all-too-apparent challenge: but having evolved, it manifestly will not simply dissolve with the overcoming of that challenge. Such an extended and sophisticated machine has many uses other than military ones, and its effect on economic development when peace is won is likely to be explosive. Will it traverse the same paths in spoliation of the human and natural environment as its opponent? There is surely ground to doubt this. To begin with, it will commence reconstruction in a context in which the gross environmental ill-effects of American military technology will be major problems, and this will have the result of stimulating an unparalleled conservationist effort. To switch this on and off at random will prove quite impossible: and since the will to rehabilitate the habitat will become a national priority, it will obviously affect the development plans which follow. If Korean experience proves anything, it reveals the astonishing productive potential we may anticipate in Vietnam: the evolution of both countries will require close monitoring by socialists and environmentalists alike during the coming decade.

D

In the light of such studies, there may well be strong grounds for doubt about some of the more overtly Malthusian assumptions of ecological theorists. As a general commentary on these ideas, we could do worse than recollect Engels' account of the controversy of his own time, set down in his famous letter to Kautsky:

'There is, of course, the abstract possibility that the number of people will become so great that limits will have to be set to their increase. But if at some stage communist society finds itself obliged to regulate the production of human beings, just as it has already come to regulate the production of things, it will be precisely this society, and this society alone, which can carry this out without difficulty. It does not seem to me that it would be at all difficult in such a society to achieve by planning a result which has already been produced spontaneously, without planning, in France and Lower Austria. At any rate, it is for the people in the communist society themselves to decide whether, when, and how this is to be done, and what means they wish to employ for the purpose. I do not feel called upon to make proposals or give them advice about it. These people, in any case, will surely not be any less intelligent than we are.

'Incidentally, as early as 1844 I wrote (*Deutsch-Franzosische Jahrb.*, p.109): "Even if Malthus were altogether right, it would still be necessary to carry out this (socialist) reorganisation immediately, since only this reorganisation, only the enlightenment of the masses which it can bring with it, can make possible that moral restraint upon the instinct for reproduction which Malthus himself puts forward as the easiest and most effective countermeasure against over-population." [6]

Engels' last paragraph has a particular relevance to

our own discussions: for sure, capitalism has survived (for twenty years? . . . fifty years? . . . seventy years?) longer than he anticipated, and its ecological crisis *would* demand structural changes before remedies could be forthcoming, even if it were to prove far less severe than Professor Ehrlich thinks. Exactly *what* population can be maintained in post-capitalist India, or Indonesia, is clearly a matter for some study, and we should certainly not dismiss the idea that this is a far more pressing problem in 1972 than it was in 1881. At the same time, we should equally certainly not dismiss the idea that the liberated ingenuity and creativity of millions of Indians or Indonesians can still exercise a powerful and positive effect on the final terms of the equation, when they come to be elaborated.

While my own bias would be towards considerable scepticism about the meaning of population projections, for the reasons I have given, which imply that China may well support more millions still if need be, while Africa and Latin America will scrimp and starve far lesser population increases, simply because restrictive social conditions prevent people from finding ways to help themselves: nonetheless it seems to me that there is one key area in which the ecological debate compels socialists to take careful stock of their basic theoretical equipment. This concerns the problem: what constitutes a *need*? If everybody *needs* to fly in Concorde, then they can't: that seems superabundantly plain. We shall drink up all our oil in short order if only a proportion of the world's VIP's come to the conclusion that this is amongst their urgent necessities. The notion that everyone in the world needs a car presents a similar problem. With somewhat less clarity, we can see a whole series of like difficulties looming up when we look at the likely availability of useable resources in a number of other fields. This appreciation must require at least some intellectual effort by socialists about their fundamental goals.

The classic statement of the socialist aim is that of Karl Marx:

> '. . . after the enslaving subordination of the individual
> to the division of labour, and therewith also the an-
> tithesis between mental and physical labour, has
> vanished; after labour has become not only a means of
> life but life's prime want; after the productive forces
> have also increased with the all-round development of
> the individual, and all the springs of co-operative
> wealth flow more abundantly—only then can the
> narrow horizon of bourgeois right be crossed in its
> entirety and society inscribe on its banners: From each
> according to his ability, to each according to his
> needs!'[7]

This celebrated watchword has a very plain meaning: bourgeois right will be superseded when society has de-veloped to the point that it can sustain the free personal development of its members to the point that each makes voluntarily his own contribution, which represents the best of which he is capable, in the light of his *personal* estimate of his ability: while each receives according to his needs which, in the context, can only be those which are felt, subjectively, to exist. In this sense alone can we make sense of Marx's own view that, for him, communism represented a step beyond the realm of necessity.[8]

Marx had written about 'a first phase' and a 'higher phase' of communist society, and had given his view that the reign of subjectivity would begin in the higher phase, with the final abrogation of 'bourgeois right'. His schema was substantially modified in the Soviet Union after 1934, with the announcement of the inauguration of 'socialism' at the conclusion of the farm collectivisation programme. The full socialisation of property was identi-fied as the consolidation of Marx's 'first phase', and a new principle was announced as relevant to this: 'from each according to his ability, to each according to his *work*'. This formula is a subtle modification of that of Marx. 'Work' is not a quality which is evaluated purely subjectively: on the contrary, for a vast majority of workers in the Soviet Union it can be very precisely assessed, and quantified, according to what are claimed to be 'objective' criteria. True, there is the age-old problem of arriving at a calculus which can permit estimates of the relative worth of physical and intellectual work: and the Russians have reached no deeper into the heart of this difficulty than have the industrial psychologists of Western capitalism. Indeed, Elliot Jacques' nostrum of a 'time-span of responsibility' which would pay people according to their capacity to operate without supervision, for all its manifest logical shortcomings, seems a severely practical measure compared to those applied in the USSR, when things are no better advanced than they were in the division of labour between Sidney and Beatrice Webb at the turn of the century. 'Sidney' said Beatrice, 'is responsible for the matters of fact in all our researches, while I am in charge of matters of principle.' 'Who, then,' asked a curious disciple 'determines which is which: what is fact and what is principle?' 'Oh' came the reply, 'that is a matter of *principle*, and so it is bound to be my concern.' Somewhat similarly, the calculation of the relative value of mental and manual work in Russia appears to be quite squarely and definitively the responsibility of mental workers. Hardly surprisingly, Mme Furtseva's salary has thus been estimated to reflect far greater social effort than that of a coal-miner. But if 'work' is in truth difficult to evaluate objectively, it is certainly evaluated *externally* as far as the operative is concerned. At the same time, the word 'ability' bears a very different meaning when it is juxtaposed with 'work' than it held when it was linked with 'need'. Marx thought of ability in the same way that he thought of need, as a quality subjectively assessed. But just as whole batteries of work-study men can with greater or less degrees of apparent justice pin cash amounts on units of work performed, so, in such a context, 'ability' becomes an externally adjudged, and therefore, to a degree, externally limited, matter. This gross devaluation of the socialist goal reached beyond the initial verbal modifications of 1934, to culminate in the revision of the Russian Communist Programme at the 22nd Congress of the CPSU. In the discussion of this Programme, which marked a considerable departure from Marxist orthodoxy, N. S. Khruschev made it plain that under communism the phrase 'to each according to his needs' certainly did not mean 'that each individual could claim just what he liked.' Since the new society was due by 1980, this was a provident reservation, even if it might have drawn a blistering criticism from the author of the *Critique of the Gotha Programme*.

Yet, if communism in its classic literature is about the rule of 'subjectivity', at no point did Marx reject the view that in all human society individual personality is developed in social interaction. 'Needs' for him, were largely learnt behaviour. Describing the formation of needs under capitalism, he was extremely specific on this matter:

'Our needs and enjoyments spring from society: we measure them, therefore, by society and not by the objects of their satisfaction. Because they are of a social nature, they are of a relative nature . . .'[9]

Under capitalism, this relativity takes competitive forms:

'A house may be large or small; as long as the surrounding houses are equally small it satisfies all social demands for a dwelling. But if a palace arises beside the little house, the little house shrinks into a hut. The little house shows now that its owner has only very slight or no demands to make; and however high it may shoot up in the course of civilisation, if the neighbouring palace grows to an equal or even greater extent, the dweller in the relatively small house will feel more and more uncomfortable, dissatisfied and cramped within its four walls.'[10]

Does this mean simply that Marx thought everyone must keep up with the Joneses? Hardly: he was concerned to illustrate the extent to which appetites are evolved, beyond simple natural needs (whatever they are) to increasingly *social* conventions. Two post-Marxian insights need to be taken into account in updating this intuition: first, the extent to which the creation of needs has itself been institutionalised, in the development of a specific industry concerned with advertising and marketing. This is one-sidedly considered, from different sides, by Fromm in his book *The Fear of Freedom* and by Marcuse in *One-Dimensional Man*. Secondly, there are artificial social limits to this learning-process, which have come to be explained in conventional sociology by the concept of reference groups. Some such concept is needed to account for the fact that in all our cities slums and palaces have been jostling side-by-side, in narrowly adjacent districts, for a century or more, and yet incendiaries from the poor districts are extremely uncommon in the rich ones, while expropriations of the mansion-holders and penthouse dwellers are almost unheard of, except as hippy escapades. However we may wish to develop these later ideas, there will be few people who wish to resist the basic notion that men learn their needs in social interaction.

The debate on the environment raises the possibilities of a studied attempt by authority to intervene in this process for 'social' purposes. In this connection there is already a developed arsenal of techniques not only in the advertising business, but, from another side of the problem, in the institutions of the welfare state. The danger of elite pressures for the control of 'anti-social' appetites and the 'social' manipulation of needs is all too painfully apparent. We could well reach a situation in which a managed or 'concerted' capitalism developed an ideology of need-control which was not a thousand miles in its assumptions from the surrogate-communism of Mr. Khruschev. It is for this reason that socialists who are alive to the problem of environmental development need at the same time to pay close attention to the refinement of their own concepts, not in order to dilute them, but in order the better to insist on the democratisation of all those areas of decision-taking, extant and about-to-come-into-being, in which these considerations are going to figure. If it becomes plain on investigation that this or that resource will largely disappear in ten or twenty years, the labour of adapting to such a problem must be a truly social, truly collective one, and not a response by a narrow interest group. No such decisions can be taken collectively without open and public argument, since no such decisions are without differential ill-effects on different social groups. The more true it is that there are serious resource problems, the more necessary it becomes that strict social accountability be imposed on every authority involved in access to those resources. The graver the threat of pollution, the greater the concerted social effort required to meet it, and the more profound the need for democratic means to arouse the conviction that the effort is necessary. And the larger the problems of adaptation to new natural imperatives, the more need for creative involvement by wider and wider sections of the affected population.

Industrial, political and social democracy are not, in

this sense, dispensable attitudes, transitory systems of administration. They must be at the very core of any strategy for the defence of man's environment, if we are not to see a situation in which the very squalor of capitalism becomes a pretext for riveting its basic institutions and impulses even more firmly and inflexibly on an increasingly reluctant society. In reaction to the spoliations of capitalist industrialism, nineteenth century socialism developed a set of ideals in which the generous impulses of men could once again recognise themselves. If these impulses are to be curbed by a new authoritarianism, if capitalism is to seek ways to enter a Spartan age where the vicious dogmas of Malthus have the force of law, then not only will we see a painful restriction of human appetites, but we shall almost certainly lose the battle for the environment as well. To state the prospect is to show how unthinkable it is.

First published in 1972

FOOTNOTES

1. Cf. Michael Barratt Brown: Must We Build More Cars and Dishwashers Before We Can Have More Roads, Schools and Houses? *Spokesman No. 12*, May 1971.
2. Professor Kapp was introducing his paper at the Fourth I.G. Metall International Conference: 'The Quality of Life', held at Oberhausen, Germany, during April 1972.
3. *Capital*, Volume I, (Torr Edition) pp.513-4. Cf. also Volume III (Kerr, Chicago), where Marx claims that
   'the whole spirit of capitalist production, which is directed toward the immediate gain of money, contradicts agriculture, which has to minister to the entire range of permanent necessities of life required by a network of human generations." (page 724) and the same volume, pp.944-5. Marx also made a number of other references to the problem in his *Theories of Surplus Value*, the third and final volume of which has recently appeared, and which contains a rudimentary index.

4. Cf. *Greek Science* by Benjamin Farrington (2 volumes, Penguin, 1949) and the same author's *Head and Hand in Ancient Greece*, Watts, 1947.

5. Cf. David Ayalon *Gunpowder and Firearms in the Mamluk Kingdom*, Valentine, Mitchell, 1956.

6. Engels' letter to Kautsky, 1 February, 1881. Reproduced in *Marx and Engels on Malthus*, edited by R. L. Meek, Lawrence and Wishart, 1953, pp.108-9.

7. *The Critique of the Gotha Programme*, Foreign Languages Publishing House, Moscow, n.d., p.22.

8. Of course, Engels tells us that freedom is the recognition of necessity, an aphorism which has caused no little confusion. In this insight, 'recognition' has a peculiarly Hegelian meaning, and can only be adequately understood in the light of Hegel's own dictum 'to understand is to *pass beyond*'. [In fact, the motto originated with Spinoza, but was taken up by Engels in *Anti-Duhring*.] Lenin certainly saw all this when he annotated Hegel's *Logic* during the early months of the First World War, and wrote in its margins 'Freedom = Subjectivity'. [Cf. Lenin's *Philosophical Notebooks*, contained in Volume 38 of the *Collected Works*, F.L.P.H., Moscow.]

9. *Wage-Labour and Capital*, in *Karl Marx, Selected Works*, Vol. I, Lawrence and Wishart, 1946, pp.268-9. Richard Silburn and I have discussed this insight in the context of modern research in our Penguin Special: *Poverty: The Forgotten Englishmen*.

10. Op. cit., p.268.

6

Needs

The two related crises which have received a great deal of attention in the ecological debate raise the whole problem of popular participation in social planning to a new level of urgency. Both the acute depletion of certain non-renewable resources, and the aggravated difficulties of pollution and waste, have combined to cause men to question, ever more insistently, two things: the wisdom of allowing market forces to determine, unfettered, the rate of use of a scarce natural patrimony; and the implications of permitting entrepreneurs to cite the market as their alibi in order to avoid accusations of the systematic misapplication of materials, to say nothing of people. However, even before the recent growth of concern about the human environment, the demand for large extensions of democratic power was already becoming urgent.

During the postwar years, the growth of State intervention in the administration of privately controlled economies, with the concomitant increase in both publicly controlled enterprise and welfare provision of public services, has created large sectors of the advanced economies which are not necessarily crudely subordinate to market pressures, and which can, indeed, exert certain modest counter-influences within society, from time to time adversely affecting the free operation of the market. The result of this encroachment, however tentative and hesitant it may have been, has been a notable revival of concern with the concept of need, as distinct from the conventional economic notion of demand, which had dominated social thinking while the rationality of the market remained virtually unchallenged.[1]

The imagined sovereignty of 'demand' is obviously linked with the hegemony, or desired hegemony, of the market over all socio-economic decisions. The conventional distinction between 'effective' demand and its implied ghost, 'non-effective' demand, which would be sheer nonsense within any strict interpretation of market-based economics.[2] Since the market must necessarily produce recognition of the human or social inadequacy of such models. It has long been generally recognised, for instance, that market forces alone will never meet the housing needs, or the health needs, of large sectors of the populations working in even the most successful market economics.[2] Since the market must necessarily produce an unequal distribution of income and wealth, there are always within its sway larger or lesser groups of people who lack the resources to translate some of their basic needs in these and other fields into 'effective demand'. Hence the growth of public provision, and of watchful underdog pressure groups in all the major economies. Orthodox economists were not always blind to these difficulties, and Marshall, for instance, troubled himself with the distinction not only between 'necessities' and other commodities, but also between the 'necessities of efficiency' and the necessities of existence.[3] But whilst all necessities were either provided in the market place or not at all, this remained an abstract preoccupation, and 'need' was condemned to seem a phantom idea outside the writings of utopians and socialists.

Today, in the self-styled welfare states, the existence of a large infra-structure of local authority housing at more or less subsidised rents, of a free or poll-tax contributory health service, of extended facilities for public education, has revitalised the awareness of 'need' in distinction from, and often as opposed to, 'demand'. The Seebohm

Report in Britain, for instance, gave semi-official status to the idea that 'the personal social services are large-scale experiments in ways of helping those in need'.[4]

Yet what *is* need? In the arguments of the current poverty lobby, and above all of the writers associated with the Child Poverty Action Group, there has been a consistent tendency to stress the learned nature of individual needs, and to worry away not only at Marshall's distinction between necessities of different kinds, but also at that between necessities and what other conventional economists call 'comforts' or even 'luxuries'. Undoubtedly the material basis for such a sustained intellectual offensive has been the non-market area of publicly provided social security.

A French study has made an effort to quantify the growth of this public sector of need-provision. CREDOC, the Centre for Research and Documentation of Consumer Affairs, identified three kinds of need: *elementary needs*, such as food, clothing, toiletries, etc; *environmental needs*, such as housing, leisure, transport; and *'needs related to the person'*, such as education, sports, health, cultural provision. They then attempted to aggregate the expenditures in each category which were made in the open market, the costs of freely provided public services, and those other costs which were refunded by social security services.[5] Their findings offer an interesting perspective on the subject:

	1959		1970	
	Collective Share	Private Share	C/S	P/S
Elementary	00	100	00	100
Environmental	10	90	12.5	87.5
Person	54	46	68	32
All Services	12	88	19	81
	= 100		= 100	

Of course, many questions remain to be asked within this framework. We cannot assume that these expenditures are uniform for all social groups, and the variations between one group and another can tell us extremely significant things about the social structure concerned.

What remains very plain is that public provision, taken at its own valuation, has different motors from market-oriented production. Commonly the social services 'create' or 'discover' needs which hitherto had never been imagined by the governors of society, and possibly not even by some of the beneficiaries of the process. In the field of adult education, poor as it is in endowments, this is a truism. But it can also be held relevant in many other areas. In the newly formed British National Health Service, the original heavy demands for false teeth and spectacles triggered off a celebrated public controversy, once these items became freely available. It was argued at the time that this rush for aid reflected the privation previously imposed by the system of market provision on those too poor (or too mean) to exercise 'effective demand'. But in a similar way, the elaboration of medical technology constantly creates new and newer needs, some of them involving far more investment than teeth and glasses. No one could 'need' a kidney machine until there was one.

An interesting example of this process is to be found in the case of speech therapy. Roughly half a million people in Britain stammer (0.8% of the population). It has been calculated that perhaps 400,000 of these people are seriously afflicted. There are 900 full-time and 500 part-time speech therapists. A recent enquiry, published in the *Guardian*, asked 30 Local Education Authorities how many adult classes they held for adult stammerers. There were three adult evening classes, two in Lancashire and one in the South of England. As Mr. Muirden, the author of this study, points out:

'This educational development is, therefore, in the hands of local stammerers and potential tutors, who must come out of their individual nonentity and organise themselves into a recognisable body.'[6]

'Need' that is to say, is not merely learned by imitation and diffused by social osmosis: awareness of it can be consciously communicated, the more so when remedies are on hand, but also to some extent when they are technically possible even if not actually available.

Yet this raises vast problems about the allocation of scarce resources. Nottinghamshire County Council recently attracted serious adverse criticism when they appointed a teacher who was subsequently denigrated as a 'Pocket-money Advisor' to organise consumer advice for children in schools. The appointment was, of course, open to debate: although some at least of the consumer groups would have welcomed it. The question is, by what criteria should such decisions be made? How does one hitherto unrecognised 'need' secure priority over another? Who decides, subject to what community controls?

Gunnar Myrdal, in his interesting study *Beyond the Welfare State*,[7] points out that the institutions of welfare in the West have grown up in a democratic environment in distinction from the mechanisms of planning in the USSR and other communist governed countries, which came into existence in the context of an authoritarian political framework. Unfortunately, the soil in which welfare has grown does not mean that it necessarily retains democratic properties itself. We have hardly succeeded in rendering the public social services democratic in themselves, either in the sense of asserting direct popular participation in, and control of them; or in the more fundamental and indispensable sense of subjecting them to effective and satisfying detailed public accountability.

Part of the problem can be seen in one of the most

interesting studies of the taxonomy of need, published in *New Society* by Jonathan Bradshaw.[8] Bradshaw is rightly concerned about the amorphousness of the concepts of need, and in an effort towards clarity separates four distinct definitions:

First, he identifies the idea of normative need, which may be summarised as the bureaucratic determination, by an administration of social scientists, of minimum levels of adequacy. These norms may be matched by remedial provision, or they may not. Examples he offers include the British Medical Association's nutritional standard, or Peter Townsend's 'incapacity scale'. Much progress has been made in defining such norms in the fields of housing and education during recent years.

Secondly, he recognises *felt* need, as the stated wants of those for whom services are offered.

Thirdly, he lists *expressed* need, or demand (not in the economic sense) in which lacks will provoke actions, demanding a service. Examples he offers include hospital waiting lists, or possibly, housing waiting lists.

Finally, he accepts the idea of *comparative* need, in which either persons or areas are compared with others, and found to lack amenities which are generally accepted as necessary elsewhere.

Bradshaw then goes on to offer a model connecting these different concepts which can interrelate those more or less precise measures of need which may be elaborated on the basis of each taken individually. The important thing about this whole valuable exercise is that it is oriented at planners and policy-makers exclusively, to enable them to refine and evaluate their judgements. And it is exactly this 'need' of the planners which demonstrates how far our services are from being able to live up to Gunnar Myrdal's expectations about their 'democratic' content, since effective participation and consultation would by themselves produce notable refinements in most public plans, as well as allowing planners to educate themselves in the process.

The relevance of this problem to the wider ecological issues, demanding as they do significant extensions of planning, both in order to eke out scarce materials, to research and develop substitutes, and to clear up and prevent mess, should be evident. Democratic forms of society will be increasingly difficult to maintain unless we can effectively extend the principles of social accountability and direct popular participation in decision-taking into what are, at present, either authoritarian and technocratic preserves. Naturally, this is not to argue against the development of technique, now more urgent than ever, but to argue for its application under genuinely democratic controls, in response to democratic initiatives.

At this point, one must obviously consider the tools which are available for such controls. The growth of governmental and local administrative organs, voluntary organisations, trade unions, and pressure groups certainly provides us with a confusion of institutions. What is required is not simply a refinement of organisational forms, still less a proliferation of offices, but an enrichment of the simple traditional constitutional doctrine of separation of powers, such as might prove possible once we began to take the notion of accountability seriously. Any genuine separation of powers exists to prevent the concentration of authority in a manner harmful to civil liberties. Bitter experience, in a succession of countries, reveals the peril of minimising the importance of the continuous extension of such checks and controls, to render them relevant and effective to cope with the enormous (and up to now, largely necessary) growth of bureaucratic administrative forms.

In its pure form, this problem poses itself most clearly in the 'socialist' societies, in which planning is unimpeded by the institutions of private property, yet in which democratic initiatives are as yet markedly limited and, indeed, restricted. This has been perceptively understood by Mihailo Markovic (the Yugoslav scholar who was dismissed, with his colleagues in the Belgrade School of Philosophy, after an unprecedented governmental campaign which culminated in an arbitrary decision by the state authorities of Serbia to overrule the University's statutes. At the beginning of 1975, against the will of their colleagues, the Belgrade philosophers were suspended from teaching duties).

Markovic argues[9] that the doctrine of separation of powers needs now to be consciously applied to information and communication services, so that not only raw data, but also access to competent, and if necessary, adversary, technical advice, should become available to groups of citizens as of right, for whatever social purposes might seem relevant to them.

In capitalist economies, the resistance to such doctrines has a dual root, in contrast to the single, bureaucratic-political source of limitations on information flows which control the communist states. Capitalist societies encourage a certain dissociated pluralism in the communications media, and in the fields of intellectual organisation: although they have given rise to a modified bureaucracy in both local and national Government and their out-stations, which is not without its East European parallel. But the major obstacle to freedom of information is still, in such societies, undoubtedly located in the institutions of private property, which require that not only material producer goods, but certain kinds of knowledge, be restricted to more or less exclusive proprietorship. To establish truly universal access to knowledge would be to negate the domination of resources by particular interests: and it is this salient fact which has encouraged the industrial demand for accountability, commonly pursued under the slogan 'open the books'.[10]

Needless to say, this is not to argue that universal access to knowledge *can* be achieved without other prior material changes: George Orwell pin-pointed this question with characteristic clarity when he wrote that: 'Until they become conscious they will never rebel, and until after they have rebelled they cannot become conscious.'[11] While the problem is confined solely to human consciousness, it is insoluble.

In industry, the grass roots urge for access to information has been reflected in official programmes adopted by both the British Labour Party[12] and the Trades Union Congress.[13] The whole strategy of 'planning agreements', as devised in the Party's industrial policy statements, was originally conceived as a two-way squeeze on private monopolies of information, from trade union and Governmental sides respectively.[14] Companies would be compelled to disclose certain whole categories of information, both to the state and their own employees (through the unions), thus facilitating both collective bargaining and tripartite planning decisions. In the event, the Wilson administration discreetly withdrew from the honouring of this commitment, but, instead, adopted parts of the institutional framework which had been proposed by the Labour Party in opposition, carefully filleting this of the real powers which had been intended for it.

But whilst the Government has chosen caution, the grass-roots organisations of the trade unions have shown increasing belligerence on this question. One of the main by-products of the movement of factory occupations, which began at Upper Clyde Shipbuilders, was the development of the notion of the 'social audit'.[15] Originally canvassed as a response to pit closures during the 1960s, this idea came to life in a most spectacular way, w[...] the Scottish TUC convened an extended public[...]

into the overall socio-economic effects of the proposed closure of the shipyards. Naturally, the balance sheets of UCS provided many arguments for closure. But, taken in conjunction with the social costs of unemployment, rehousing and renovation of industrial potential, these arguments became much less convincing. A wider accounting framework posed questions which could never even be asked within a straightforward calculation of profit and loss within the shipbuilding industry itself. Even excluding the moral costs of closure, which is itself a moral choice which may or may not be justified, the simple cash costs of social security benefits and redevelopment could, when carefully computed, provide powerful evidence for maintaining an otherwise 'unprofitable' concern in being. The example of the Scottish TUC was subsequently emulated in a number of other threatened enterprises. At the River Don Steelworks in Sheffield, white-collar and production workers combined to produce a blue-print of the effects of closure proposals which aroused widespread concern amongst industrialists who were British Steel Corporation customers, and resulted in effective pressure for a stay of execution. By the time that the 1974 Wilson administration took office, this kind of reasoning had taken root very widely, and the new industry minister, Mr. Tony Benn, found it perfectly possible to encourage its more general application.

Confronted by a widespread liquidity crisis, British industry was facing a particularly difficult time. Not only were there bankruptcies and closures of plants on a wide scale, but a number of transnational companies were brought to the point at which they decided to close all or part of their British production potential, and to opt for attempts to hold their previous market shares by importing products from their overseas plants. Tony Benn greeted the workers' representatives who beseiged him for Governmental help in these situations with a novel proposal: he commissioned independent consultants to prepare feasibility studies under the control and guidance of the relevant trade union bodies. This innovation was applied in cases such as the closure of Imperial Typewriters' factories in Leicester and Hull: [16] it stimulated the unions into complex efforts at alternative planning. Not only did they have to argue with qualified professionals about the possibilities of continued or modified production in the plants concerned: they were also powerfully motivated to examine the overall performance of their former employers, to document the investment and marketing programmes which had produced their present adversity, and to seek to arouse public discussion on the social priorities involved.

The demotion of Mr. Benn after the result of the EEC referendum was not sufficient to prevent the continuance of this type of approach. When Chrysler Motors announced their closure plans towards the end of 1975,[17] the instant response of the shop stewards was to replicate this example, in a most careful and imaginative way. Perhaps the most dramatic example of the social audit at work is to be found in the extraordinary initiative of Lucas Aerospace workers,[18] who, encouraged by Mr. Benn, prepared a detailed blueprint for the transfer of their industry to 'socially useful and necessary projects'.

Naturally, the social audit has, until now, remained mainly a labour of self-education and, in a sense, propaganda. But it is not difficult to see the potential which it contains as an instrument for democratic planning. By putting experts to work for oppositional groups, it calls in question the prerogatives of managers and professional planners, and ends the monopoly of initiative.

If the welfare sectors of our economy were to learn from these experiments, they could rapidly extend their innovative capacity in a very real way. If the social audit is relevant to productive effort, then its correlative in the field of social consumption would be the 'needs budget', or inventory of social demands.[19] There is nothing to stop local authorities, or welfare agencies, from initiating an open and continuous discussion upon the question of which needs should have priority, and how scales of priority would be determined. This could enfranchise all the welfare pressure groups, and bring them into an organised effort to evaluate the relative importance of their own particular claims on public resources. As things are, most bureaucracies calculate their future development in terms of x per cent expansion across the board in favourable times, and y per cent cuts during the lean years. A rudimentary jockeying can take place between departments, but it is no secret that the outcome of this is frequently determined as much by the personal capacities of the jockeys as by the comparative urgency of the needs upon which they ride. If needs budgets became as general a feature of the work of such agencies as their normal revenue and expenditure accounts, then the process of popular consultation and discussion which would be involved would itself constitute a real resource, which could itself help to expand the material means which were available to solve specific problems.

In the middle run, such democratic advances as the social audit and the needs budget will prove themselves necessary if there is to be any future for democratic political forms in general. The capitalist industrial powers have advanced half-way to democracy, but if there is not a continued forward movement there will be a retreat. Half-and-half autocracy and self-government is no permanent mixture: it is, in our situation, an impasse, in which government of any kind, leave alone self-government, becomes increasingly impossible.

If we are to consider that the debate on the environment has warned us of real hazards, we must anticipate attempts to discover authoritarian solutions for them. The alternative, which perhaps begins with the kind of tentative reforms outlined here, will see needs as growing in an increasingly self-aware social process, and will seek to meet them by recognising their combined personal and social identity. This task could never be begun outside an ever-expanding democracy.

First published in 1976

FOOTNOTES

1. Cf. notably Peter Townsend: The Meaning of Poverty, reprinted in his collection *The Social Minority* (p.35 et seq.) Allen Lane, 1973. Also two essays by the same author in *The Concept of Poverty*, Heinemann, 1970.
2. Recently this recognition has been extended, as city governments themselves have met mounting financial pressures. Cf. Theodore W. Kheel: *The Quality of Regional Development—The Case of New York*, in *Qualitat des Lebens*, 6: Europaische Verlagsanstalt, Frankfurt 1972.
3. Alfred Marshall: *Principles of Economics*, Vol. I, p.122. See also Charles S. Wyand: *The Economics of Consumption*, Macmillan N.Y., 1937, Chapter 5.
4. Even so, the Seebohm Report provided no satisfactory definition of 'need'.
5. Bernard Cazes: *Planning for the Quality of Life in Mixed Economies*, in *Qualitat des Lebens*, 7: Europaische Verlagsanstalt, Frankfurt 1972.
6. Ronald Muirden is Tutor in Stammering Correction at the Addison and Central London Institutes, and author of *Stammering Correction Simplified*, (J. Garnett Miller Limited, London).
7. Duckworth, 1960. Cf. Chapters 7 and 8 especially.
8. 30th March, 1972. No. 496, pp.640-3.
9. In an as yet unpublished paper to the American Philosophical Society, 1975 Convention.
10. Cf. Michael Barratt Brown: *Opening the Books*. IWC Pamphlet No. 4, 1968.
11. *1984*, Penguin Edition, p.60.
12. The Labour Party: *Report on Industrial Democracy*, June 1967 and *Labour's Programme*, 1973.

13. TUC: *Interim Report on Industrial Democracy*, 1975: and *Report on Industrial Democracy*, 1974.
14. See Stuart Holland: *Strategy for Socialism*, Spokesman Books 1975, pp.62-76, and the same author's *The Socialist Challenge*, Quartet books 1975, chapters 7, 8, 10 and 11.
15. Michael Barratt Brown: *UCS: The Social Audit*, IWC Pamphlet No. 26, 1971.
16. *Why Imperial Typewriters Must Not Close:* IWC Pamphlet No. 46, 1975.
17. Joint Union Declaration of Chrysler Shop Stewards and Staff Representatives: *Chrysler's Crisis: The Workers' Answer*, December 8th 1975.
18. Lucas Aerospace Combine Shop Steward Committee: *Corporate Plan, 1976*, published by E. F. Scarbrow, Hayes, Middlesex.
19. Cf. my paper The Social Audit and the Inventory of Social Needs, in *Community Development Journal*, OUP, Volume 8, No. 3, October 1973.

7

The Case for Consumer Democracy

In their evidence to the Bullock Committee, which is examining the TUC's proposals for the reform of company structure, the National Consumer Council suggests that, if unions are to be represented on company boards, then consumers must be represented as well. The council echoes Sidney and Beatrice Webb in suggesting a tripartite system of government for nationalised industries, involving 'consumers, employees and management': and they suggest that if Lord Bullock recommends in favour of union representatives on the supervisory boards of ordinary companies, then they will need to campaign for similar facilities for consumers. This view seems to have influenced Ronald Butt, in his discussion of workers' control (*The Times*, April 29, 1976).

Advocates of industrial democracy will tend to agree that any balanced reform of the industrial power structure must augment the effective powers of consumers: although few would now defend the proposals of the Webbs as offering any practical advantage either to individual consumers or to effective management. Yet undoubtedly, those of us who wish to see an extension of workers' control have a responsibility to think through the problem of the defence of consumer interests.

In order to do this, it is necessary to question the assumption, shared by Mr. Butt and the National Consumer Council, that industrial democracy necessarily amounts either to 'syndicalism' or neo-syndicalism. The weakness of anarcho-syndicalism as a model for social organisation was that it sought to enfranchise labour by giving over the government of industry and society to industrially organised unions, which, it proposed, would administer industry within a market framework. It was difficult to see how this arrangement could facilitate either social planning, or the development of social forms of consumption.

The current rediscovery of the ideals of self-management and workers' control, takes place in a context in which the negative lessons of omnipotent state bureaucracy are completely plain to read, while the western capitalist economies have evolved very large welfare sectors practising highly social forms of distribution (as in the health and education services, where there already exists in several countries something close to distribution according to need); and a variety of experiments in indicative planning, some of which, with the aid of devices such as planning agreements, could actually be transformed into effective prescriptive planning mechanisms, subject to a high degree of democratic accountability. In this situation, the key weaknesses of syndicalism are considerably limited, if not entirely overcome. In great measure, we have in planning structures the solution to the problem of representing firms in their capacities as consumers.

If consumer democracy is to become real, in the form of personal powers as well as collective ones, it seems urgent to look at a wider range of democratic approaches than are involved in simple representation. Direct representation is possible wherever there are constituencies close-knit enough both to constitute an electorate and provide an active and continuing public opinion capable of influencing, and holding accountable, such representatives as are chosen. A coal mine, for instance, is exactly comparable with the units which seemed logical to the Greeks for the practice of democracy. But coal consumers fall into two categories: on one side, the large customers, pre-eminently power stations, and, on the other, a dwindling band of personal users of solid fuel. The first category of consumers are certainly compact enough to be involved in the National Coal Board, although they are likely to find their interests better served if adequate inter-industrial planning machinery can be evolved. The individual coal burner, however, is a constituent of a territory so amorphous that it is impossible to see how he could be democratically represented. How could he vote, and how would his delegate discover his views? Does this mean, therefore, that he may have no demo-cratic rights or influence? Not at all.

The device which he needs to develop will be an ex-tension of the old constitutional doctrine of the separ-ation of powers. He needs access to objective information, and the means to contribute his own information, includ-ing, of course, complaints, to the stock of such knowledge. The dissemination and collection of such information, needs to be organised, and kept as rigorously separate from executive authority as the judiciary, and yet it needs to have inviolable rights of access to the facts which are relevant to it. Free public opinion will sooner or later do the rest. If *Which?* reports that a given car is twice as costly and half as efficient as its competitors, then its manufacturers, whether they are organised in autocratic or democratic units, will have to pay attention. If the consumer defenders report that a given toy is dangerous to children, then the lobby can even, if necessary, seek legislative action to prevent its distribution. The principle can be extended to the point at which consumers feel that they are satisfied: and today 'consumers' may include numbers of socially conscious and quarrelsome defenders of the environment.

Direct representation would, of course, be eminently feasible in the area of social, as opposed to individual, consumption. Already we have lay governors of schools, and public nominees serve in the controlling bodies of a variety of welfare agencies. Yet, even in this sector, perhaps the doctrine of separation of powers has greater relevance than the mechanism of representation. If our major public services were compelled to operate a public, open, and active needs budget, involving an ongoing institutionalised discussion between all the relevant pressure groups, then not only could priorities be rationally tabled and independently assessed, but quite possibly considerable scope could be given to stimulating voluntary efforts within the public sector with an advisory needs budget were part of the local government mechanism, such problems would be ventilated, and the process of accountability would be markedly improved.

In short, if we want to apply democratic norms to economic institutions, we have far more scope than might be thought by those who confine themselves to the narrow agenda suggested by the issue of representation. Workgroups can and should be served by representative forms of government: but that government need be no less constrained by overall democratic pressures than any other. An industrial democracy will need to carry the doctrine of separation of powers to hitherto undreamt of limits.

First published in 1976

8

Is Socialism Possible?

How does it come about that for a hundred years trade unions have been primarily concerned with 'a fair day's wage', only at rare moments bursting through *en masse* to approach the demand for the 'abolition of the wages system'? In what possible ways might we expect this demand to become a practical one, when it has been generally forgotten for years? Might we expect to see the whole problem discussed again, in similarly speculative terms, in another hundred years' time?

There are good reasons for thinking that the answer to the last question is 'no'. To understand these reasons we must examine the difficulties raised in the first question. The most popular explanation offered up on the left at the moment is a rather vulgarised version of Lenin's theory of a 'labour aristocracy'. Simplifying Lenin's subtle formulae, it is assumed that imperialism, colonial and monopolistic extortion, has enabled the metropolitan ruling classes to cast 'crumbs from its table' to favoured sections of the working class.[1] The latter are thus bought off, given high hopes of reform and persuaded to settle for such reformist solutions to their complaints. In this bald form, the theory has some disadvantages. For one thing, the most militant and aggressive sections of the trade union movement in almost every advanced country are the better-paid ones. It was the skilled engineers (pushed, it is true, by the threats of mass-production techniques to their skills, but joined by mass-production workers in their response to these

threats) who formed, in England, that nucleus of the shop
stewards' movement, in the First World War, which became, directly, the main working-class base of the young
British Communist Party. In most Western countries, and
especially in Germany, Italy, Belgium and Hungary the
same thing is true. In Spain, today, the leaders of the
recent strike wave are not the most poverty-stricken, but
the best-paid workers.

One must immediately make the point that if it made
sense to describe Lord Carron as a labour aristocrat, this
was not by virtue of his nurture in Section One of the
Amalgamated Engineering Union, the section catering
for skilled craftsmen: on the contrary, it was by virtue
of his *political* role that he secured preferment, became
a member of the Governing Board of the Bank of
England, a Papal Knight, and collected a whole series of
similar honours. The same thing applies to that small
but potent cadre of trade union leaders, members of parliament, and professional publicists who, from the heights
of the Labour movement, come to seem worthy of occu-
pying various positions of state. If one studies the salaries
paid to trade union officers, one quickly discovers that at
the lower ranks these are frequently less than those of
many of the employees they represent, while at the higher
levels there is no tight correlation between amount of
salary and political fidelity to the objects of the movement.[2] Some of the best paid general secretaries are
among the most authentically militant, while some of the
worst-paid are among the most abjectly deferent to authority. It is the opportunity to take up positions of influence and prestige within the established state and
industrial power-structures, *not* crude ransom, which
marks off this particular aristocracy. Certainly, the elev-
ation of trade union barons to say nothing of their employment in sundry necessary tasks of State, has been an
increasingly frequent spectacle since the war.[3] No doubt

all of this contributes to the stilling of unquiet trade union consciences, and the restriction of the vision of significant groups of leading Labour personalities. In turn, this reinforces and multiplies the pressures to conform to more and more limited patterns, to strive for less and less general reforms, to accommodate and to succumb.

Yet the temptations which are offered to Labour leaders are quite distinct from those offered to the working class itself. A skilled man in the car industry who earns an above average wage is in no way tempted by this fact to make peace with his employer. On the contrary. His earnings are more likely to be seen to depend upon militant vigilance.[4] And so among these workers one finds the most vocal and sustained opposition to the powers of employers; while among the more depressed, and therefore, more apathetic, workers, life may be patiently sustained on disgraceful wages.

If the 'labour aristocracy' is seen as a *political* outgrowth of this kind, it must clearly be *explained*. While it is not improper to look for the thirty pieces of silver which may be involved in the business, these will not account for the fact that it was transacted. How does it come about that in a hundred years of history, during which huge mass political and trade union forces have been assembled, there has never arisen the kind of self-confident mass-power which could control its leaders and avoid the transmutation of overall socialist goals into increasingly nugatory marginal reforms?

When Marx offered the advice that 'a fair day's pay' was a conservative slogan, he indicated the direction in which we should search for evidence about this. Workers suffer exploitation, alienation. The machines they make, ever more complex, are ranged against and over them ever more tyrannically. Capital, a social power, accumulated labour, is concentrated into private hands and in them deployed against the living labourer. Workers may react, as we have shown, by various personal expedients, involving withdrawal, recalcitrance, dissociation. Or, when the opportunity presents itself, as it inevitably and recurrently must, they may associate. Joining together helps them to protect themselves. It extends over each individual an awareness of identity with others in the same position. It distils the recognition of *interests*, as opposed to monadic appetites. 'We' become separate from 'them'. But the goal of self-protection, of mutual defence, does not automatically give place to that of social fulfilment, of radical attack.[5] The will to rule is forged with difficulty. True, a band of men may more easily work out, collectively, estimates of the causes of their discomfort than single isolated individuals; but collectivity, while conducive to thought, does not automatically bring insight. Although all thought is a social process, and ideas are inevitably sparked into life in dialogue between men, none the less they achieve their expression through individual heads. And the heads are not equally well-placed to transmit them. This is not for one second to concede that differences in 'innate intelligence' can explain the differences in human attainment: even if such a reactionary supposition seemed true, we should need to declare war upon it, to rebel like Prometheus and discover means by which to overthrow such an order of things. But at the moment we need no such supposition, because there exists a far more obvious explanation for human inequality, in the existence of the division of labour. As Adam Smith remarked, the difference between a philosopher and a porter is far more easily explained by the use which has been made of their faculties than by the original state of those faculties themselves.[6] Men become good for what they are expected to be good for. Thus it makes sense to explain the difficulties which workers experience, in comprehending the root causes of exploitation, by reference to the division of labour itself. In our society, the habit of abstract thinking is coalesced into determinate occupational strata, while physical activity is lumped on to other, separate, shoulders. Comprehension of the State, the market, and the other totalising concepts which are vital to the generation of an attacking, aggressive political strategy, is not so easy if you have been kicked out of school at the age of fifteen, perhaps without having been taught the names of the five continents, and certainly without having been inducted into any of the more abstract mental disciplines. For a mineworker or a busman, until he has worked hard and long on political and economic problems, thought tends to move around concrete practical happenings and impulses.

It is little more than an appreciation of this fact which is involved in the insistence, by Kautsky and Lenin, that 'socialism must be brought to the working-class from outside'.[7] Certainly this does not mean that socialism can be manipulated into being by gifted pedagogues: what it does signify is that mental work, in capitalism, tends to be done by mental workers, and socialist ideas, like all others at this time, tend to find their systematic exponents among people with a training which has been acquired outside the working class. Certainly the notion of alienation cannot occur in any human head which has not begun to conceive of a notion of integrated human community: both require a high level of abstract intellectual activity. That every human being can, potentially, participate in such activity is an elementary axiom of socialism. Less elementary, but no less axiomatic, is the appreciation that it is the 'mind-forged manacles' of man, of commodity-fetishism, which are the principle obstacles to such universal understanding.

It is too easy for socialists to forget that capitalism is the *given* system: the climate. Its customs and standards are the *normal* rules: it sets the boundaries to men's con-

ons of what is 'natural'. If you are prepared to try experiment, it is possible to buy a pair of spectacles ch will invert your image of the world. For a little while, everything will appear upside down. However, should you persevere for long enough, you will find yourself adapting to the new condition, to such an extent that, should you revert to ordinary spectacles, they in turn will turn the world upside down all over again for you. If our senses can adapt to the tricks of the physical world, so our morality may all too easily adjust to the exigencies of our social world. It is not, it need hardly be said, 'natural' for men to produce capital which promptly contributes to their enslavement. This is a peculiarly social act, particular to special kinds of society. But if this inversion of the moral world is 'normal' it can also come to seem 'natural'.

Fortunately, at the same time that it evolved this strange state of mind, Capital also evolved the conditions in which men could challenge it. It developed not only the moral atmosphere in which it became possible for men to dream about community, but the physical powers capable of sustaining such a community in reality. But, as we have already argued, while standards of this kind are extremely abstract and general, the lives of the workers are in every sense practical and particular. If a moralist can reason from abstract principles back to particular cases, a worker will normally build outwards from immediate experiences to the general. If the division of labour promotes a social schizophrenia, it crystallises at the same time both poles of the field of this argument: while it gives rise to the 'stabilising' myths about present social reality, it also unleashes 'disruptive' truths which may yet come to undermine it. Pursuing this logic, we see that workers organise themselves in shops, in factories, before they extend their links to embrace a firm or combine: and on the basis of solid achievement at local level, they put out their powers to form organisations at industrial, national, and even international levels. But socialism is a world view, distilled from the most intellectually adventurous, most profoundly humanist insights of the capitalist and preceding eras. It is at the historical intersection of these ways that we can see Marx, who read through Aeschylus every year, talking to a body of English artisans who had banded together for the achievement of a 'fair' wage.

'Fairness' remains a key conception of the trade union movement to this day. Although, formally, Marx's appeal has won over numerous trade union organisations, which have been for a long time committed to 'the overthrow of the wages system', at least in the unread preambles of their rule books, it is still true that the nearer one gets to the grass roots, the more important 'fairness' becomes. The Nottinghamshire miners have coined a word for this ethos: 'fairation': it is used as the standard of what is tolerable and what is not. The last strike which involved any significant part of the coalfield took place during the war, when a miner's son was balloted, under the Bevin scheme, for conscription into the pits. Fairation was outraged. Loyal miners, who had never complained when innumerable rods had been laid on their own backs during the depression, rushed to stop work. The established code, which included every father's hope that his own son would escape the life that he himself had suffered, proved to have an imperative force that no simple and direct personal wrong could equal. But on a smaller scale, the idea of fairation is invariably involved wherever any pronounced injustice calls for remedy. Men will stop work to secure fair treatment for a worker who has been victimised, or for a team which has been underpaid, when they themselves have no immediate monetary interest at stake. 'Fairation', or some similar conception, is the watchword of the overwhelming majority of militant actions, whether they concern wages or not. An increasing number do not.[8] But what should be clearly understood is that however defiant or intransigent the defence of fairation might be, it does not at all necessarily connect with any move to reject the values and priorities of the given system. The same work-people who may well be fiercely involved in battles for 'fair' treatment might even be numbered among 41.7 per cent of Labour voters polled by Colin Hurry and his associates in 129 marginal constituencies (in 1959) who wanted 'no more nationalisation'.[9] Their uncertainty about nationalisation would certainly be linked with a lack of conviction that it is 'fair'. The old and tired question, 'How would *you* like it if you built up a shop, and the government came and took it?' is asked by far more workers than most socialists are willing to admit. The reason for this refusal of the Left to face facts stems from a naïve assumption that democracy is about counting up the opinions of the people. It is not: it is about liberating their energies and opening their horizons to the widest human limits. Majorities for us can never be merely counted up; they must, as Trotsky once said, be *won over*. Distorted though Hurry's findings are likely to be, they are less inaccurate than the preconceptions of many people in the labour movement. Of course, a blastfurnaceman who invokes the sanctity of property in sweet shops when discussing the nationalisation of the iron and steel industries has got the wires crossed. The same sense of 'fairness' which might cause him to react with ferocity against the victimisation of a workmate can, when stretched beyond the frontiers of his own immediate grouping and over boundaries of class, become a dulling, neutralising and mystifying force. It is this dual notion of what is fair that must collapse if Capital is ever to be subordinated to human, social control.

If the fundamental system of present values is contradictory, there can be no continuous valid standard of what is fair. It is perfectly fair, within capitalism, for Capital to seek to maximise its returns. To do this, it is not only fair but necessary to seek to buy labour at the cheapest possible price consonant with productivity. It is equally fair, within the same framework, by the same ethics, for Labour to seek for itself the highest possible return. 'While there is a free for all, we are part of the all', says Mr. Cousins. But more than this is true. The rights of Capital, here, and the rights of Labour, there, confront one another, head on. There is, as Marx pointed out, an antinomy, right against right. 'Between equal rights, force decides,' he added.[10] To force, we might add cunning. And cunning has been largely concentrated at one corner in this century-long combat.

The task of the socialist movement is to break down the power of these standards, of the enslaving and de-moralising notion of 'fairness' within an unfair system, of the assumption that it is 'natural' for men to be displaced from a livelihood because it is 'normal' for the results of public effort to be privately appropriated.[11] This task has to be consciously carried out. If it is not, however sharp and strong the reactions against specific complaints, however heroic the struggle for fair treatment, none of the preconditions for structural change are created, and the mind-forged manacles may never be removed. In such a situation, however far the individual leaders of the labour movement may be able to see beyond capitalism, they will have no force to get there. So it is, in this climate, that men who once burned for freedom grow accustomed to the narrow vision and the comfortable perquisite. Labour aristocracy, such as it is, grows up in the climate of commodity fetishism, of the domination of men by myths, in which inanimate property seems to radiate with its own malign will, while men themselves become objects, without responsibility or power.

How, then, may we move to overcome these difficulties? If it is right to look at the notion of fairation in
order to meet them, we come to some fairly simple conclusions. First of all, it is not enough to take the two
slogans which Marx discussed. Between the idea of a fair
day's pay and the goal of the abolition of the wages
system, it is clearly necessary to place a third demand.
This, anchored to fairation, and acceptable within the
logic that prevails, leads to the understanding that nothing short of a new structure, a new social order, will meet
the workers' aspiration to a fully human status. Too
often, in the past, socialists have set their policies at an
earth-bound level of mundane reform, and their dreams
in the heavens. A minimum programme is elaborated, in
which it is promised that no man shall any longer endure
a leaking roof. A maximum programme is hinted at, in
which it is hoped that 'men to men the world o'er shall
brothers be for all that'. Between the two yawns a vast
gulf, a vacuum which is quickly filled by perfidy of a
thousand kinds, small-minded moralising, sermons, disillusionment, prayers and manipulation. The process has
never been more starkly apparent than today.

The search for intermediary, transitional objectives is
one which presents continual difficulties. Almost every
demand which is capable of unifying a group of people
in actions to realise it has a transitional element in that it
generates solidarity and a sense of corporate identity. But
solidarity will become attenuated, and collective attitudes
subordinated within the dominant culture if one vital
question is ever omitted. That question is the question of
power. Fair wages may never, by the very nature of the
wages system, be attainable; but a spurious, if temporary,
sense of attainment is possible from time to time whenever demands are limited to purely monetary matters.
The one central area in which demands for fair treatment
cannot in the nature of the case be contained and subli-

mated is that of power, of control. This demand constantly recurs in trade union activity, although it inevitably starts at the level of the factory or workshop, and only with difficulty puts out wings to embrace industry at large, the economy as a whole. None the less, increasingly insistent calls have been coming from the factories in recent years, and there are numerous signs of serious attempts to generalise them.[12] If the instinctive moves of shop stewards to pose the call for control, with even greater urgency, at factory level, can be co-ordinated and extended to their logical frontiers, then around the cry for workers' control can arise a new movement which may prove capable of transforming the whole social framework.

In this, the development of capitalist organisation itself is helping to break down the old mental barriers. Halt, lame, though they may be, the movements by capital to 'plan' in an indicative sense; the ever-growing dependence on self-financing methods; the forcible moves towards state control of wages, and the relentless attempts to pare away trade union rights: all combine not only to anger the labour force, but to teach it old lessons in a new and easily understandable form. Increasingly, the old struggles about the distribution of rewards between labour and capital within particular firms, the traditional attacks by fragmented sections of trade unions upon the profit levels of individual concerns, are being brought into doubt by the actions of neo-capitalism itself. More and more, workers are compelled to dispute about the distribution of the *national* income, about the global return to *social classes* as such, about the size of the whole sector of wages and the scope of the whole return to capital. To the extent that the new ideology of 'planning' takes root, the old claptrap about 'rewards for risk' becomes self-defeating. All these processes may, if there can be created a vital and aggressive socialist movement to exploit them, help to settle the fog, to dispel the protective myths and enable people to see the moral world the right way up. As this happens, the very arguments most confidently employed by the apologists of the present state of things are turned against them.

At the same time, the implication of the Labour Party leadership in the forlorn struggle to revivify the British economy on a neo-capitalist, technocratic basis presents its own challenge to socialists. The more entangled the old leadership becomes in rationalisation projects aimed at restoring some version of the old structure, the more it loses conviction for its supporters. It is this key problem which demands an answer before we can move towards a real solution to the other difficulties we have considering.

First published in 1967

FOOTNOTES

1. Lenin's most important remarks on this question have been republished in the compilation *V.I. Lenin against Revisionism* (Moscow, 1959). The most significant remarks are contained in the tracts: *The Collapse of the Second International; Imperialism, The Highest Stage of Capitalism; Imperialism and the Split in Socialism;* and *A Caricature of Marxism.* In the above edition, see especially pp.257-76; pp.292-346. Also the excerpt from *'Left-wing' Communism—An Infantile Disorder,* p.35. For an interesting recent discussion of the matter see Michael Barratt Brown, *After Imperialism* (London, 1953), especially the introduction and chapters 3 and 4 (pp.80-150). Also Ernest Mandel, 'After Imperialism?' in *New Left Review,* 25 (May-June 1964), pp.17-25. Of course there is an enormous difference between the sociology of the labour force in the period we are discussing, and that of Victorian times. cf. Royden Harrison, *Before the Socialists* (London, 1965).

2. The 1958 salaries of national leaders of the AEU rose between £910 and £1,180. Even with an expense allowance, these would have seemed extremely low in ASSET. Although some right-wing unions have been both extremely undemocratic and at the same

time lavish with their rewards to their leaders (e.g. the National Union of Seamen, which until recently paid the General Secretary a salary of £2,000 per annum *tax free*), many more have been relatively democratic and at the same time fairly mean with their key leaders. For a discussion of this topic, see Clegg, Killick and Adams, *Trade Union Officers* (Oxford, 1961), pp.55-91.

3. Clegg et al., ibid., p.85. Out of 266 fulltime officers who had resigned from office, this team tracked down 48 who had taken jobs in nationalised industries, 25 who had received posts in home and colonial government service, 14 who found places in private industrial management, 4 who took up work with the Labour Party, and 4 who became MPs. 13 others went back to the shop-floor. For a discussion of honours, see V. L. Allen, *Trade Union Leadership* (London, 1957), Chapter 1: The Ethics of Trade Union Leaders; on the acceptance of State honours, see pp.30-9. See also the Report of the General Council to the TUC, 1959, concerning the restriction of opportunities for trade union leaders on the boards of nationalised industries. Few more eloquent appeals have been heard from this body.

4. For discussion of this, see 'Men and Motors' by Dennis Butt, in *New Left Review*, 3 (May-June 1960). This article was based on extensive discussions with J. L. Jones, then Midlands Regional Secretary of the T & GWU.

5. This problem was closely analysed by Perry Anderson, in 'The Origins of the Present Crisis' in *Towards Socialism* (London, 1965), pp.30-47.

6. *The Wealth of Nations* (London, Everyman ed., 1910), p.14.

7. Lenin, *What is to be Done?* (London, 1929), pp.39-44. In this Lenin follows Kautsky's line of argument completely; basing himself on an article by Kautsky in *Die Neue Zeit*, XX, 1, 3 (1901-2), p.79. (Both thinkers use the word 'ideology' in a neutral sense, to mean a 'coherent body of ideas', rather than what Marx and Engels meant by it, that is, 'false consciousness'. However misleading, and—by later standards—wrong this might be, in the view of Marx and Engels it may yet be 'historically necessary'. This means that both Kautsky and Lenin were, here, 'revisionist' in orthodox Marxist terms, and it should be added that their treatment of this problem does not benefit from this.)

8. About half the strikes which take place nowadays concern matters of 'control'. In 1964, for instance, a breakdown of strikes by stated causes ran as follows:

Principal Cause	No. of Strikes	No. of Men Involved	No. of Days Lost
Claims for increase	540	293,000	786,000
Other wage disputes	686	111,300	267,000
Hours of Work	23	12,500	37,000

E*

Demarcation disputes	61	17,400	37,000
Disputes on employment or sackings	263	61,900	285,000
Other Personnel questions	80	19,900	77,000
Other working arrangements	765	145,000	321,000
Trade Union Status	98	18,500	174,000
Sympathetic Action	26	21,300	27,000

Linking those causes (bracketed above) primarily concerned with control questions and challenging managerial prerogatives, we get:

On control issues	1,206	245,300	857,000
All Strikes	2,524	833,000	2,277,000

(Source: *Ministry of Labour Gazette*)

9. *Nationalisation; That Survey*, by Colin Hurry and Associates (London, 1959), p.23.
10. *Capital*, vol. 1 (London, 1938), p.218.
11. 'We are not installing £4 million of equipment in order to employ the same number of men. We can't carry people for fun.' So Mr. Alan Dick was reported as saying in May 1956 after the declaration of widespread redundancy at Standards. Similar attitudes are ten a penny. More and more frequently, though, the £4 million is raised *internally,* from the firm's surplus, without the intervention of a halfpenny of outside capital.
12. See Tony Topham, 'Shop Stewards and Workers' Control' in *New Left Review*, 25 (May-June 1964), pp.5ff. and my own 'Democracy and Workers' Control' in *Essays on Industrial Democracy*, Spokesman Books, 1971.

9

Socialists and the Labour Party

'What, then, is it reasonable to expect from the Labour Party in the years ahead?

'There are two entirely opposed ways of answering this question. The first proceeds from the view that the Labour Party, whatever its past and present shortcomings, can eventually be turned into a socialist party, genuinely committed to the creation of a radically different social order, which would be based on, though not exclusively defined by, the social ownership and democratic control of a prominent part of the means of production, distribution and exchange, including of course the "commanding heights" of the economy. The second view is that it cannot be turned into such a party. Of the two, the second seems to be much the more realistic.'

With these words, Ralph Miliband opens the concluding section of his new[1] postscript to *Parliamentary Socialism*, a work which has deservedly achieved the reputation of a classic, as is witnessed by the remarkable frequency with which it is paraphrased and restated, often shorn of its finer nuances, in the columns of the radical socialist press. The book as a whole has been improved by updating: the same postscript contains a pithy, yet entirely convincing, account of the abysmal epoch which has become known as the 'Wilson years'. Certainly it would be difficult for a socialist to disagree with Miliband's findings, in this scrupulous balance-sheet of that dismal time. But do such findings merit his conclusion? I think they do not, because I think they reach far wider, and have far more serious implications than he seems to believe. If the Labour Party cannot be turned into a socialist party, then the question which confronts us all is, how can we form a socialist party? If we are not ready to answer this question, then we are not ready to dismiss the party that exists.

It is no use at all to claim that the dispersion of illusions about the Labour Party will produce a climate in which new organisations may take root: for that is not the way that established parties are disestablished in developed political structures. Only when an alternative has already emerged can masses of people change their allegiance in any permanent way. In Britain this is particularly true: it was not by accident that the Labour Party grew up in the shade of the Liberal Party, gradually (and, for a long time, by no means unequivocally) distinguishing itself in the process. People facing immediate political problems don't just withdraw into a wilderness in order to take counsel with one another and decide what to do next, while people who don't face such problems aren't in political organisations anyway. This is true in any functioning and generally accepted democratic system, although of course, in a structure which is seen and felt not to be democratic, things are somewhat different. Since the collapse of the Independent Labour Party, there has been no group of socialists in Britain capable of maintaining a full-scale political presence outside the Labour Party.[2] By a full-scale presence, I mean the ability to secure the election of at least a handful of members of Parliament, the ability to present a strong oppositional challenge at least in a certain number of local councils, and the ability to maintain a visible base of organised trade union and community support. That numerous groups have been able to develop short of this capacity is quite obvious, and that many of them do not aspire to this kind of presence is equally clear. But unless their aspirations change, as indeed they might if circumstances made it rational for such change to set in, such groups will not play a macropolitical role. They may influence particular actions, and gain support in certain sectors of the population, but they will not become vehicles for the development of the outlook of a whole social class until they can be seen to have the potential to enable that class to speak for itself at every political level on which its interests are the object of contention. Even the corporate interests of the subordinate class cannot be safeguarded without organisation on this scale: and it is manifestly silly to speak about 'hegemonic' aspirations developing within such a class unless it has safely passed the point at which its self-defence is relatively assured.

And this is why socialists cannot ignore Parliament. The lesson becomes clear if one takes as an example the non-marxist, or at any rate non-Leninist, radical socialist responses which have bloomed during the years of the Wilson apotheosis. It is convenient to consider two of these. The first takes the form of community action, on a local scale.[3] Tenants' associations, residents' committees, bodies airing and voicing the complaints of whole populations on council estates, in ghettoes or slums, or bodies aimed at particular groups, such as the Claimants' Union which attempts to organise people living on social security, the unemployed, and strikers claiming benefit: all such bodies can draw upon a very real store of grievances. But how are such grievances to be dealt with? Let us take the example of a slum area, in which widespread poverty exists alongside very poor housing, and numerous problems caused by neglectful or absentee landlords, or Rachmanism. Such an area will experience numerous tensions: it will have high rates of delinquency, and it may well be an area in which prostitution is to be found. At the same time, it will place in juxtaposition poor 'respectable' families, Methodists or

Catholics, so-called 'multi-problem' families, and a succession of waves of immigrants of various nationalities. Uniting such a population in any action at all is difficult. But it can be done, on particular issues: against Rachmanism, or in favour of play-streets, or for pressure on any one of a variety of social welfare agencies. Most of the questions which are within the scope of local authorities may, at some time, give rise to successful community action groups. But how must a *socialist* view such action? Of course, he will support anything which increases the solidarity and self-confidence of working people and their dependents. Yet, having said this, the community action group has frontiers which positively preclude any real struggle for betterment, unless it is linked with a *political* movement operating on the scale of the whole given polity. Slum-clearance? Yes, this is possible: you can make the local authority rehouse everyone, although this is difficult. But when you do, your rent will be trebled or quadrupled, because the authority will build houses on expensive land, at high cost, using funds bearing extortionate interest rates. Cheap houses, or dear houses, are a matter of alternative governmental policies. Higher wages? Well, you can pursue them through your union, if you have one, and if it is strong enough to help you, and if there isn't a freeze or standstill. Even this avenue leads to a need for alternative governmental policies. Better schools, improved transport, more amenable social services are all partly approachable by lobbying to change the priorities of your town council, but will all result, at best, in deteriorations in others' amenities unless Governmental policies are changed. So what consciousness can be aroused in such struggles will remain *sectional* unless it is keyed into an embracing political strategy involving *all* the poor, *all* the ill-housed, *all* the deprived.

The other non-Leninist approach to gain wide currency

partly appreciates this problem. It consists of the development of specialised pressure-groups acting precisely for all the poor, or all the ill-housed. The Child Poverty Action Group, or Shelter, are typical cases in point, much to be supported and admired, but suffering from a crucial weakness nonetheless. Each makes the best case it can on its theme, but each can only remain effective while it narrows its scope, for each is limited at all times to the need to pressurise the political system as it exists, by influencing personnel who have every reason to reject any overall attack on the linked constellation of problems which have been separated into single issues for the purposes of the lobby. See the challenge as it is, with all its ramifications, and, once again, you will face the need for an integrated political movement with a coherent set of policies across the board.

None of this argues a *priori* that Parliament could be the effective vehicle for successfully implementing such a set of policies. That question will never be finally answerable until the experiment has been tried, in a context of such an intensity of external agitation as may be realisable. What it does argue is the much more fundamental case that consciousness of class, in the full sense, as opposed to sectional militancy and local activism, crystallises around the demand for exactly such a programme, which consists not primarily of a set of potential Bills, to be enacted by 350 victorious Governmental delegates, but of an alternative view of society for the mass of the people, a peep at new potentialities and an awakening of aspirations not on a sectional or regional scale, but at a level understood by the whole active part of the subordinate class. Once such visions have been evoked then the socialist movement will be in a position to resolve the ancient Reform/Revolution dilemma, but before then the whole question is almost as remote as that of the nature of the Holy Ghost. Revolutionaries who attempt to set up the barricades against the wishes of their wonted supporters will not prevail. Indeed, we can be sure that the wishes of the working class will define themselves, in the first place, as demands on the given structure, not because of any universal reverence for the dignity of Mr. Speaker, but because sectionalism can only be transcended when all eyes are turned in the same direction, and the given structure is so shaped as to ensure that there is only one direction to which all eyes *can* be turned at once.

That is why politics, which should never be reduced to Parliamentarianism, will not, in England, readily be separated from Parliament. It is for this reason that few, if any of those people who are equipped to understand Miliband's book are in fact presently engaged in attempting to bring about the alternative party organisation which he desires to see. His most sympathetic readers will readily confess, if pressed, that they have no idea how a new socialist party could be brought into existence.

There are, of course, many socialists who feel that they do have the answer to this problem, although Ralph Miliband himself is not to be numbered among them. At a rough count, there must be several thousand socialist activists in Britain who have banded themselves into what they usually regard as Leninist organisations, which bodies, by the time the Wilson administration came to an end, had already proliferated to the point that they could be counted in dozens. Several of these groups represent quite serious assemblies of talents: two, the Communist Party and the Socialist Labour League, are able to produce daily newspapers, which is a feat of organisational skill and dedication that appears totally beyond the powers of the Labour Party itself. At least two more produce weekly journals: one, the *Socialist Worker*, claims a readership in excess of that commanded by the organ of the traditional Labour Left, *Tribune*; while the other, the *Militant*, has been growing steadily and exercises considerable influence on the Labour Party's youth movement, through which channel it has secured the election of one of its spokesmen to the Party's National Executive Committee. Other lesser groups produce fortnightly journals such as *Socialist Fight*, irregular ones such as the *Red Mole*, or monthlies representing a variety of Trotskyist, Maoist, and other revolutionary opinions. No one should dismiss this burgeoning of socialist argument and organisation, but at the same time, it is difficult to avoid the conclusions that a great deal of it is peripheral to the real political concerns of working people, that some of it is abstract and doctrinaire to the point of self-parody, and that although there *are* some exceptions, there are few indeed among the leaders of these currents of thought from whom we may expect either concern for the practical unity of the working-class movement, or rigorous intellectual work of a standard sufficient to advance its cause, leave alone examples of that fused revolutionary praxis to which we are constantly exhorted but seldom shown the way. It is perhaps indicative of the intellectual difficulty in which this fragmentation finds itself that from nowhere within it has come a book which even remotely approaches the stature of Miliband's own study of the Labour Party. As a dedicated and scholarly independent, Miliband can keep his eye on the main scene. But for many of the activists of the organised left groups, factional warfare preponderates over all other activity whatsoever. From within the disciplined ranks of all too many of these, split succeeds split with bewildering rapidity and expulsion inexorably follows each inevitable deviation, so that all but the most disembodied fellow travellers are so busy watching for the theoretical knives which may, any day, divide their own shoulder-blades, and few can have time to notice what is really happening in the world outside.

It is true that there have been repeated attempts to link these quarrelsome splinters into one all-embracing movement. In the late fifties, Walter Kendall and Eric Heffer both made attempts to persuade them to sink their differences, when at a time when the Trotskyist and syndicalist groups numbered perhaps 1% of their present adherents, they brought most of them together for a series of abortive conferences on unity. The result was failure. More recently, in the mid-sixties, the May-day Manifesto called all who would come to its banner, and stayed in business for long enough to publish at least one admirable text and to encourage a worthwhile growth of community action groups and women's liberation caucuses.[4] However, all too predictably, not only did that initiative fail to produce the intended fusion of energies and efforts, but indeed its prime movers themselves succumbed to the very fission against which they had been pledged to act. This pattern has repeated itself on the fringes of the British Labour Movement so frequently that it surely deserves analysis. It should be said at once that such analysis must begin with the appreciation that the fringe is an important place, not simply an irrelevance, and with the recognition that since 1968 the socialist groupings of the far left have contributed to an unprecedented upsurge of interest in socialist ideas, which has already filtered far deeper into the structure of the Labour Movement than any previous socialist revival. Yet for all that, evolving as it has at a time of unparalleled intellectual bankruptcy in the central councils of the official Party machine, it has largely secluded itself into a ghetto of its own making, so that its practical influence on the policies and personnel of the major unions, and of the Labour Party itself, is greatly less than might have been expected.

Part of the reason for this is to be found in the nature of the half-truths which have played an important role in

exacerbating the divisions of the far left. It is true, as
Miliband has continually insisted, that there can be no
purely parliamentary approach to socialism, and that the
Labour Party has always failed to develop anything like
a campaigning strategy to mobilise extra-parliamentary
action when it has been needed, even if it has been
needed to uphold the freedom of Parliamentary choice
itself.[5] But it is not true for a moment that this implies
that socialists should ignore parliament, which remains,
for all the real powers which have seeped away from it,
a focal point of continuing importance for the development of a more widespread political understanding. It is
true, as all the revolutionary groups insist, that capitalism, if ever threatened, will put up the strongest possible
resistance, by whatever means it has to hand, to prevent
its own extinction or harassment. But it is not true that
this inevitably means that the scenario of St. Petersburg
1917 is the scenario of London in 1984.

It is certainly true that there will be no development
of socialism without a prior development of socialist
ideas, and that these demand both organisation and intellectual discipline. But it is not at all true that the socialist
ideas which are appropriate to defeat late capitalism were
all formulated, intact, fifty or a hundred years ago.

It is true that the working class movement has suffered,
throughout Europe, years of timid and purblind leadership during which elaborately fortified bureaucracies have
developed in all major labour organisations. But it is not
true that such bureaucracies are impregnable, or that
such leaderships are irreplaceable, and even if it were
true, they would need to be opposed and fought on their
own terrain if ever they were to be defeated.

It is true that West European Labour has much to
learn from the history of the revolutions in Russia and
China, and something to learn from many other examples,
most notably that of Vietnam. But it is not for one

moment true that the sociology of the decadent imperial metropolis is reducible to that of these models, or that the forms of political organisation appropriate in their conditions can simply be transplanted bodily and set to work to liberate Germany or Scotland. It will not escape the student of revolution that the differences between the Russian, Yugoslav, Chinese and Cuban revolutions are at least as important as their similarities.

It is above all true that socialism is an international movement, which needs a functioning international organisation, co-ordinated action, and a developed exchange of ideas and information between adherents in different countries. But it is equally untrue that such an organisation can develop fruitfully without the rapid accession of that degree of material and moral authority which comes from the incorporation of real sectors of working-class opinion in a number of national centres simultaneously, since international action requires serious numbers of supporters if it is to be effective, and ideas which cannot produce action we already have in abundance, which is one of the things we are complaining about.

It is obviously implied in all this that we need to study Marx, Lenin, Luxemburg, Lukács, Trotsky, Gramsci, Mao and many other great figures in the history of socialist thought: but it is equally implied that we need to think for ourselves, and that this is a most difficult task to perform in the manner required to help ordinary workpeople in their struggles, if we remain artificially disengaged from all the major problems which confront the working-class movement, as it is constituted at present, in the organisations which it has evolved in the attempt to meet those problems.

The major assumption, underpinning all the other half-truths which have crystallised the fragments of the New Left, is the assumption that the present crisis is, before all else, a 'crisis of leadership'. If only the working-class were properly led, this argument runs, then capitalist society, already rotten-ripe for replacement, would be restructured in short order. Connected with this view, and meshed into it, is the theory of 'labour aristocracy', put forward by Lenin on the basis of various remarks of Engels as an 'explanation' for opportunist politics in Western Labour Movements. The most finished statement of this view was furnished by Trotsky, in his famous 'Transitional Programme'. This is a work which contains a number of absolutely crucial insights, first among which is the appreciation, conveyed in the popular title of the work, that the conventional social-democratic and communist view of a disjunction between 'maximum' and 'minimum' programmes is acutely disruptive of socialist consciousness. The two halves never fuse, and for the very good reason that reform programmes are conventionally structured within the realm of possibility which remains open in the given social order, and so have nothing whatever to do with any overall proposals for recasting that order itself. Trotsky saw the need for a programme of immediate demands which led out of one social order into another, and about this need he was certainly profoundly right. His own actual proposals for such a programme were, however, rooted in the social conditions of the late 'thirties, which are manifestly *not* those of the postwar capitalist democracies. Indeed, both Trotsky and his followers believed the whole evolution of West European and United States capitalism in the postwar period to be foreordained: it would be short, convulsive, dictatorial and terminal. This preconception was quite false, and resulted in the prolonged atrophy of Trotskyist organisations, which were reduced to the merest handfuls of dedicated pietists for a twenty-year period, only to re-emerge to a certain minority prominence in the period of acute instability in

Russian and East European institutions which set in after
1956. One distinguished Trotskyist theorist, Felix Morrow,
did foresee, at the end of the Second World War, that
Western Capitalism could experience a prolonged stabil-
isation, in which the working-class would be best-advised
to pursue an extended programme of maximally democratic demands, effectively extending the notion of 'transitional' politics over a relatively longer period, instead
of siting them within a convulsive immediate trauma. He
was ignored.

During the same period, the notion of a Labour aristocracy became more and more obviously untenable.
Indeed, Sternberg had given Trotsky very clear statistical
evidence of the error of this hypothesis during an interview in the mid-thirties but his evidence had been dis-
regarded, perhaps because Trotsky could scarce afford to
cultivate 'revisionist' conceptions at a time when his
position was more and more isolated and vulnerable.
Heresy has its limits, as many a heretic has shown. Be
that as it may, the prolonged relative post-war quiescence
of Western workers' movements was *not* due to the fact
that they were misrepresented, but to the fact that, for all
too long, they were all too accurately represented by
their conventional labour leaders. Of course, the changes
in leadership which have more recently been evolving in
many countries reflect considerable changes in the economic position of advanced capitalism: a very significant
radicalisation directly results from the inability of late
capitalism to assuage the appetites it arouses. Even so,
in the main democracies, it is quite absurd to think that
the defence of democratic institutions has suddenly become irrelevant, and if in the 1970s there is any programme of demand which can have a truly transitional
meaning, it will be a programme of systematic democratic
advance throughout industry and society.

This requires an altogether different type of socialist

advocate from that produced in the old schools. Dedication to revolutionary models established during the first five years of the Comintern does not produce the kind of mentality which can meet the challenges of working-class democracy in late capitalist society: which is not to say that the fundamental insights of the early Comintern were all wrong, but rather that the imitative attempt to re-enact bygone historical events within a radically different context is bound to produce frustrations which all too easily result, first of all, in disenchantment with the actual workers' movement of modern times, and the consequent growth of *élitism*, substitutionalism, and then ultimately in withdrawal of those involved from the real practical political arena. There has been an acute discontinuity in the revolutionary process during our century. That the lessons contained in its books are important is beyond question: but they must be filtered through the experience of subsequent generations if they are really to be digested.

The plain reality is that, however clever individual socialists may be, they need, all the time, to listen to ordinary workers if they are ever to be of any help to them. Of course, their listening mechanisms may vary. As they develop their organisations, they may find themselves elevated to the position in which they can listen by proxy: but only if they have recruited many pairs of observant ears which have been taught to appreciate what it is they hear. Even then, this process is a difficult one, and could not have its difficulties better exemplified than by Lenin, who had to use every art to cajole, threaten and browbeat his highly-trained cadres after the February Revolution of 1917, before they could be brought into line with their constituents, to face the possibility of October.

Today, in every European country, the volatile left groups which see themselves as Lenin's successors,

although they perform invaluable work as publishing
houses, seminaries, training schools for young political
activists, are almost as bereft of applied strategic ideas,
practicable alternative policies, ongoing influence over
decisive working-class institutions, as the great brainless
dinosaurs of traditional Labour are bereft of principles,
morality or socialist orientation.

If one limits one's field of view to the domain of abstract ideas, it is apparent that the young left makes all
the running. But if one puts out of mind all interest in,
and responsibility for, the major mass-organisations, one
then confronts a somewhat barren choice: to opt for a
particular groupuscule as being potentially less exclusive,
less sectarian, less dogmatic and more hopeful than all
the others, or to continue in what has hitherto proved to
be a fruitless attempt to persuade all relevant tendencies
to regroup into a viable political formation. Neither is at
present a very plausible bet. The groups may unite, but
only if some event is traumatic enough to take them by
the scruff of the neck and make them, and then suf-
ficiently persistent to keep them together for long enough
to achieve something recognisably useful. Where events
might succeed, persons are quite unlikely to substitute.
To join together and integrate such disparate forces
requires a degree of charisma which is just not available
to any man or group of men presently in opposition to
the system of advanced capitalist society. Orpheus could
silence the birds with the sweetness of his music, but he
would undoubtedly have gone deaf in the effort to secure
a hearing in this tumultuous world. If the intellectual
giants of socialism, now dead, cannot inspire co-ordinated
effort from their disciples, how will living men succeed?
There is, of course, a way: if socialism were to come into
being in any one advanced country, its example would
clear the way to an unprecedented convergence of socialist forces in all the others. But in the meantime, such

transitory unity as may be realised before that happens is of very great value, and in general, it will result from the development of successful examples in action, which themselves are the precondition for the real advance of thought. In the beginning was the deed.

The force of this argument is greatly fiercer in Britain than in many other European countries, although, in a modified form, it is bound to apply there as well. This fact stems from the nature of the Parliamentary system in Britain, which, except in the principalities, is essentially a two-party system in which voting is to an overwhelming degree polarised on class lines. Whatever the ultimate role of Parliament in the socialist transformation of society, and about this I am even more agnostic than some of the professedly revolutionary groups, it remains profoundly true that people who can't win by-elections can't win socialism.[6] It is always possible to kick up a row, and sometimes possible to brawl in a manner which, on balance, is socially educational. But you can't win adherents to a new view of society without political organisation, and that will never leave the domain of fantasy until it is compelled to address the issues of the day, in a manner which defends and advances the felt interests of working people.

These interests can never be experienced as *interests*, rather than separate appetites or sectional demands, unless they can be generalised into some form of overall political platform. For all the deep ruminations about 'consciousness' which have covered reams of paper in socialist journalism during the years of the New Left, there have been few attempts to trace the actual movement of socialist ideas and their organic relation to institutions. This fault is particularly to be charged against the very people who have made the most noise about abstract 'consciousness', in the present circle which surrounds the journal *New Left Review*.[7] When Tom Nairn

takes issue against nationalism and in favour of the
healthy disorder of the European Economic Community,
as a catalyst of hoped-for socialist reaction, this lacuna is
made openly evident. For Nairn, nationalism is a particularly pernicious form of 'false consciousness', comparable with, say, the condition of commodity-fetishism,
as a source of mystification and support for capitalist
social forms. Leaving aside for the moment the fact that
capitalism in Europe will undoubtedly stimulate a wholesale resurgence of particularist nationalism, as capital is
concentrated to the centre, and the periphery bleeds, the
diagnosis could not be more wrong. To the extent that
the established political institutions of Europe do not
operate at the scale of the economic organisation of the
block, this will impede rather than assist the process of
crystallisation of oppositional forces. Consciousness of
class may reach out to embrace international criteria, but
it always originates within a given political structure, and
finds its primary criteria in the struggle to identify itself
against its *national* adversaries. Even when nations are
merged into supernations, as is projected in Europe, this
process will continue to apply, with two counteracting
pulls to impede its development. A *European* working-
class will evolve with the greatest difficulty, for the good
reason that opposed to the process will be, not mystifi-
catory figments, but rational choices. The first counter-
pressure will be that already mentioned, of peripheral
nationalism, which will certainly be reinforced by the
economic difficulties of neglected regions, and which will
provide a key challenge to socialists, who will need to
identify with it to the extent that it enlarges the scope for
self-determination and self-activity on the part of working people concerned, and at the same time to uphold
internationalist perspectives before it in an attempt to
subvert the world beyond the narrower new frontiers.
Irish nationalism provides one convoluted example, in

this part of the world, of the link between socialist action and national independence movements, but new examples will emerge, if the adherence of new states to the EEC is not reversed, in Scotland, Wales, and elsewhere, just as they have already emerged in Southern Italy and Wallonia. Some examples will prove negative, as has the Italian. Others will not.

The second great pull on the working-class organisations of all European States will be that of solidarity with workers and the peasant poor in the rest of the world. The contradictions in which the trade union movement now finds itself can exemplify this problem. At this time, international trade unionism is organised in two heavily bureaucratised federations, one of which has until recently benefited from funding and advice from the C.I.A., while the other has not been outside the reach of the appropriate desks in the Soviet Foreign Ministry. European economic integration raises the demand, which will become increasingly insistent, for an integrated European trade union federation cutting across both the old Cold War union structures. Up to a point, this would represent a certain advance. But then, when one confronts the recent example of Chile, one sees the disadvantages. When the Kennecott Corporation was nationalised, it began a complex process of law-suits to obtain control of Chilean copper exports. This continues. But in his speech to the General Assembly of the United Nations, President Allende[8] was at particular pains to point out that, following an appeal by Chilean unions, the French dockers refused to unload copper consignments from Chile until litigation was completed, and the rightful ownership by the Chilean Government vindicated. More and more the transnational corporations will impose the necessity for such actions, for such an appreciation of the identity of interests between workers in the metropolitan and underdeveloped areas. It is difficult to see how consciousness of 'Europeanism' necessarily conduces to such responses, if it is assumed that Englishness or Frenchness do not.

In all true internationalist actions, national consciousness is a felt reality, and must remain so until nations themselves have withered away. The Chilean upsurge itself is successful to the extent that it is a national repudiation of imperialism, and at least in this it replicates the Cuban experience. Indeed, if one wishes to see a paradigm case of the connection between the resurgence of nationalism and socialist internationalism, one only needs to look at Vietnam. If one is willing to assume that the nation is a progressive phenomenon in the third world, one has to explain why it is a reactionary event in the first world. There is such an explanation, which is to be found in the morphology of imperialism. But since Europe will be a super-imperialist state, if it ever evolves to reach the degree of integration involved in Statehood, it is hardly an advance on the beleagured and separate imperialisms of England, France, or Belgium, which have already been largely transcended by transnational companies in a new form of colonialism.

Meantime, such areas of authority as States retain, remain the focus not only of important residual powers of national capitalist classes, as yet unintegrated into a transnational class: but also of oppositional activity by working classes, even further from such integration. There will not be a European working-class in any meaningful sense until there has been such a degree of interpenetration of national capitals that it makes real sense to speak of a European capitalist class.[9] Until then, class responses by the workers should be oriented at *inter*nationalism, but will define themselves in relation to *national* challenges, *national* opponents, *national* strategic programmes.

In Britain only two established groups describing themselves as revolutionary socialists have recently attempted political action on this plane. The Communist Party loses all its electoral deposits, and is further away from success on parliamentary terms than it has ever been. This is partly because for long years of the Cold War the Communists paid for both their virtues and their vices in a prolonged political isolation. Their virtues included a dedication to internationalist principles in such terrible affrays as the Korean War: their vices included all the paraphernalia of apologetics for every act of stupidity and brutality which was performed by the Soviet Government. But in recent years there has been far less vice, and a great deal more virtue, none of which has been rewarded at the polls. Why? The answer surely, is to be sought in the complete absence of strategy in the communist electoral effort. Asked why he stands for Parliament, the average Communist candidate is in the same position as Sir John Hunt, and can only reply 'because it is there'. But while this may not be a totally silly answer in connection with the goal of climbing distant mountains, which might be thought to impose a certain degree of irrationalism on any potential contender, it is quite inappropriate as a justification for any form of political activity. And what makes matters worse is the fact that Sir John Hunt's sherpas did in fact get him and his friends up their mountain, while every communist parliamentary foray simply enriches the State to the tune of £150 per deposit lost. The real reason the Communist Party needs to go through this debilitating business is that it wants to be a serious political force, and it has been prevented from obtaining its ends in what would have been a rational way, by the means of affiliation to the Labour Party, and the election of a group of Communist Labour members. It is only very partly the Communist Party's fault that this is so, and it could with a fair measure of justice claim that it had tried to make things otherwise. However, in enforced isolation, what sensible things might Communists do about elections? Any small group with its eye on the main political developments of the day has the power to advance its cause, if it can assess its own position realistically, and act within its capacities. Since Communists wish united action with the Labour left, they could use their parliamentary interventions to achieve such a political effect. In 1970, for example, they could have run six token candidates only, against the archvillains in the Wilson administration. Or during the Common Market debate, they might have announced that they were contemplating intervention in all those seats, and only those seats, whose Labour members had lost their way in the lobbies, and that they would be particularly keen to see that wanderers from marginal seats were among the most hotly opposed. They might even have publicly reprieved such Labour members as showed themselves to be of subsequent good behaviour. In such a way, their disadvantages would all have turned to advantage, and their allies in the Labour Party would scarcely be incommoded. As it is, in every left-wing union there are recurrent squabbles about some inept intervention against a union nominee, and at least as many Labour members of the left of centre face Communist opposition as do those of the right. The whole thing is random, planless, and self-defeating. None of it goes on within any apparent wider programme of socialist strategy, whether for a renewed offensive for affiliation to the Labour Party, or for some new initiative to group socialist forces outside that Party. This is almost the worst of all possible worlds, and it ensures that whatever the merits or demerits of the Communists' programme for a peaceful transition to socialism, it remains on an entirely abstract plane.

The other group to contest a recent parliamentary election is the Socialist Labour League, which made an experimental intervention at the Swindon by-election during the last years of the Wilson government, and polled a normal vote by Communist Party standards. The League seems to be in no hurry to repeat the experiment, and has subsequently been much more concerned to angle its propaganda at Labour Party supporters than to alienate them by opposing their candidates.

There are broad questions involved in these examples. Throughout Europe there have been similar interventions by revolutionary groups in electoral contests. Indeed, the *Morning Star* reported the results of the campaign of *Il Manifesto* in the Italian elections as if they were a resounding defeat, when in fact they were very favourably comparable indeed with Communist Party performance in British elections. A marginally more successful initiative was undertaken by the French Ligue Communiste, which offered Alain Krivine as a presidential candidate. He polled 250,000 votes, and then thoroughly disgraced himself by not calling upon his supporters to go to the second round of ballots in support of the surviving left candidate. This lent justification, which was totally unnecessary, to the enraged cries of Communist leaders, that Krivine was simply a splitter and provocateur. In reality, there is no doubt that he is a dedicated and capable socialist militant: but there is no doubt either that he has not the beginning of a notion of the kind of strategy which French workers will need if they are to win the next round of political battles in which they will be engaged. That the French Communist Party can be compelled to come to terms with the forces on its left from time to time has been ably demonstrated by the United Socialist Party, and the trade union federation, the CFDT, both of whom have more than once compelled their more orthodox rivals to face issues which they would greatly have preferred to ignore. In general, though, the revolutionary left has not been able anywhere in Europe to assemble the kind of constituency which could make it politically credible in electoral terms.

There have, however, been a number of left socialist parties which have gained a certain influence during the past decade and a half. All have constituted splits in already well-established socialist or communist parties, which subsequently gathered wider support. The PSU in France is a case in point.[10] The Italian Party of Proletarian Socialist Unity (PSIUP) was another,[11] although this has recently voted to merge with the Italian Communist Party, having originally split from the Socialist Party. During its brief life, it maintained a distinguished presence in Parliament, and exercised real influence within the major trade union federation, the CGIL. But it was unable to determine a viable independent strategy. In Denmark, Axel Larsen led a significant split from the Communist Party which eclipsed its parent body in the subsequent elections and thereafter. Yet none of these organisations, varied though they have been in origin and formation, has been able to come anywhere near to supplanting the established major parties of the working class. Some attempted splits, based on nationalist currents of thought as well as socialist groupings, have achieved momentary success only to sink almost without trace. A notable example is that of the Walloon Workers' Party and the related Socialist federation in Belgium, which began with a serious trade union base, and which included among its founders one of the most original Marxist thinkers in Europe, Ernest Mandel, but which fared, if anything, worse than the broadly similar formations elsewhere in Europe.

This balance-sheet is not encouraging for anyone who wishes to repeat the experiment in Britain. Once again, it should be stresssed that all these parties have attracted many clever and self-sacrificing supporters, that all have enriched the political culture of modern Europe, and that none should be simply written off. The advocacy of Lelio Basso, of Michel Rocard, of Ernest Mandel, and of many others, has powerfully contributed to the socialist awakening which remains by far the most positive feature of the seemingly intractable territory in which we must work.

But although the creation of a renewed socialist culture is the first task of modern socialists, it will remain abstract and scholastic until it is materially embodied in working-class institutions. And the fact we must face is that once the workers' movement in any country has developed its organisations, these bodies will always stand between the articulation of any new ideas and their realisation. Unless the mass-organisations can be won over, or seriously divided in the course of an attempt to win them over, they will effectively bar the way to the emergence of any alternatives. Certainly there is no advanced capitalist democracy in which they can be simply by-passed. Only in countries in which dictatorship, or underdevelopment, or both, have left an organisational vacuum, can the new socialist ideas (or the reassertions in modern terms of old ones) come to exercise a predominant influence over the working-class through brand new organisations. Elsewhere, the material structures which have been inherited by the working population are bound to play a major role in limiting, or expanding, the political understanding which they may develop. No more obvious example of this truth is needed than that of the growth of the French Communist Party and its trade union federation, the CGT, after the events of May in 1968. Even though the French Communists emerged quite plainly as a party of order and constitutional behaviour, and though they were at pains to denounce all the most prominent inspirers of the May upheaval as disrupters and worse, and though there was at the time an absolutely unparal-

F

leled upsurge of working-class militancy and self-confidence, nonetheless the CGT followed up the return to 'normality' with very considerable gains in membership. Not for the first time, a movement which was in many key respects *against* the influence of an established workers' organisation, reacted to the benefit of that influence.[12]

It might be thought that this experience would teach the value of political organisation, of the development of a structural network of cadres and activists, even if the lesson were seen as having, in truth, some very negative implications. The same story, on a less dramatic scale, is told by the British Labour Party, which lost members on a frightening scale during the Wilson years, and entered the 1970 elections in a state of barely concealed civil war between unions and political leaders. By 1972 recruits were flowing back into the party, and both unions and political leaders were seeking urgently to discover a common basis on which to act in future. Why? Why didn't the whole alliance fall apart? The partial answer is that the Conservative Government could not have been more effective in compelling Labour's erstwhile supporters to reunite than it was, launching, as it did, simultaneous attacks on the independence of unions, the institutions of welfare, the powers of local authorities, and all those areas in which workers had been wont to consider countervailing powers as residing. Together with this fact must be taken the adjoined question we are considering: there was no practicable alternative. To fight the Rent Act, you needed Labour Councillors. Even when they collapsed under pressure, they were seen to be on the right side: and to the extent that they did not, they inspired hopes that things might change. To repeal the Industrial Relations Act, you continue to need Labour members of Parliament, since outside Ulster, Wales and Scotland no others even half-way to radicalism present

themselves as serious contenders. Labour will continue to
win certain elections while it can maintain a monopoly
of the kind of political machine which can, without un-
due strain, field 600 plus candidates in national elections
and secure support in the field for their campaigns, and
field several thousand candidates in all the main local
contests. The realities of the position become plain when
one asks, if all the groups to the left of the Labour Party
were united, could they begin to contest on this scale?
The answer is that they could not, and because they
could not, union support is bound to go to people who
can. This process alone (and it is not alone) would ensure
that the Party might possibly recover from a whole succession of Wilsons, if one considers so baneful a prospect
to be plausible. I do not consider the prospect at all
plausible, and would not exclude more cataclysmic out-
comes if it became real: but in the event of the collapse
of a structured opposition, there is no simple certainty
that independent socialists would have their field-day.
Indeed, the proven incapacity of socialism to present
itself as a practicable choice within a structured movement would not augur well for its capacities to rise to
new responsibilities in the incomparably more difficult
terrain of the collapse of such structures.

For socialist movements which arise within countries
with an existing conservatively oriented Labour Movement, there is one very clear precedent, at which these
examples only hint. Unless the existing movement is
either won over or divided, it will not be possible for
activists to develop the kind of apparatus which is absolutely necessary to meet the demands of full participation
in political life. The main example we have in this
connection is that of the greatest split in socialist history,
that which formed the Communist parties. This needed
the Russian Revolution to inspire it, and considerable
material intervention from the Comintern to consolidate

it. Even then, with all the volume of moral and material support which this revolution could offer, it miserably failed to establish effective organisations at the level we have been discussing, except in countries in which it came new, and first, to the task of organising the workers, or in countries in which it was able to detach a significant proportion of the socialist forces from their traditional organisations. In Germany, France and Italy the second conditions applied, as they did also to a lesser extent in Finland and some other countries. In Indonesia, China and Vietnam the first conditions were in force.

When Trotsky attempted to lead his supporters in a split from the parties of the Third International, he was not able to repeat this experience in any of the countries which already had developed Communist parties. The only countries in which his supporters ever maintained any prolonged Parliamentary or equivalent presence were Ceylon and Bolivia, where the first conditions we established still applied. The other Trotskyist parties all operated as minority currents in working-class movements which were already structured, and with the exception of the group in the United States, which was able to campaign for the formation of a Labour Party because there was none already on the scene, they were hardly ever able to operate on an independent scale, never mind about presenting an alternative organisation to the mass of socialist-oriented workers. If anything, the experience of Maoist groups replicates this story with even greater obviousness. Yet it would be a brave and foolish man who said that workers in, say, Western Europe, had nothing whatever to learn from either Trotsky or Mao.

Spontaneous fission, generated by the Soviet suppression of the Hungarian Revolution, or the apostasy of the Mollet socialists concerning Algeria, or the entry of the Italian Socialists to the Centre-Left government in Italy, produced the left socialist parties we have already discussed, in Denmark, France and Italy. These bodies did inherit serious forces, comparable perhaps with those of the British I.L.P. in the 'thirties. All had a parliamentary orientation, but none could present more than a minor challenge in Parliament. To succeed in their original aims they needed to have carried with them into independent action a substantial fraction of their original parties: and having failed to do this, they were bound to modify their perspectives.

So far this has been a somewhat academic argument, whose intention is to establish that the only place Ralph Miliband could find the nucleus of his opposition socialist party would be the Labour Party, and that if his new formation were to improve on the new left groups, or the left socialist models of modern Europe, or the I.L.P., it would have to detach from the Labour Party at least some major unions, and Labour activists enough to hold some town councils, and parliamentary constituencies. Doubtless, if this were done, the groupuscules would feel the pressure, and many would align themselves with the new formation.

But two questions then emerge. First, what would the new body do next, after it had emerged from the old, moribund party? If it were, however sceptically, to act on the Parliamentary plane, it would obviously require to establish a structure almost exactly on the model of its progenitor. No unions would support a new party which began by insisting on its rights to reappoint their leaders for political reasons, or to reorganise their membership on new criteria. Unions might, indeed, agree to work in a common organisation with socialist groups which did try to act on such principles, but the very least they would require would be that such socialist intervention should be governed by the same democratic processes established within the unions themselves. As long as parliamentary democracy survives in Britain, the natural form of labour

F*

political organisation will be that of a federal alliance of working-class organisations, which might well be inclusive, but which will only be integrated and led by example and the force of argument. This was the form evolved by Marx in the First International, advocated by Engels during the Second, and established on an inclusive basis by the Labour Representation Committee. That the British Marxists opted out of it was their misjudgement, and that they now remain outside it can only strengthen their opponents. The only grounds for abandoning it would be the fact or the imminent prospect of a suspension of parliamentary democracy: and it is greatly to be doubted that it could be abandoned easily then.

The reason that federal organisational forms evolved in Britain and all those other countries in which trade union organisation preceded working-class political parties is only partly connected with the need to converge upon an effective electoral presence: even the day-to-day work of labour defence requires that Trade Unions should come together in trades councils, confederal bargaining units, trade union congresses and the like. The more hotly contested the claims of the unions, and the more militant their struggles, the more call there is for integration of separate organisations in support committees and similar bodies. When the co-ops are brought into support for strikes, or when students join picket-lines, the process at work is entirely similar to that which occurs when unions combine with socialist and labour pressure-groups and organisations in order to achieve parliamentary or local government representation. The work of elaborating an autonomous political programme is not imaginable without the construction of an organisation capable of integrating the aspirations of living workers of widely different trades, skills, and interests. Of course, the socialist movement has a history, and strewn throughout this are the landmarks of a whole series of previous programmes,

from the Communist Manifesto onwards. In this situation
it becomes quite possible for isolated socialists to imagine
a platform of demands, based upon the records of bygone
struggles, distant countries, other times. Yet such plat-
forms could only have unmediated relevance to the existing, present, working-class movement by some happy
accident: in general it remains true that just as no generation entirely repeats the mistakes of its forerunners, so
no historic problems remain fixed in immobility. If we
cannot step into the same river twice, we surely cannot
coast past our present difficulties on the programmatic
demands of half a century ago.

The work of grappling with this task can only be a
work of democratic discussion. Arbitrary fiats will only
succeed in detaching and alienating larger or smaller
groups of unrepresented interests from the main force. In
any context in which the basic freedoms of association
and communications exist, even in mutilated form, the
work of organising an effective force of socialists necessarily requires an effort of convergence upon a programme, which may take the form of an alliance of existing working-class parties, where a highly structured
socialist movement exists, or which may take the form of
a federal organisation, where labour has already reached
a high level of sectional organisation, prior to the development of any integrating body of socialist doctrine. For
better or worse, this was and remains the situation in
Britain. The fact that the Labour Representation Committee lost its Marxists, who were in any event a singu-
larly dogmatic and uncreative, not to say boring, lot, at
a very early stage in its evolution, left the subsequent
Labour Party all too vulnerable to the doctrines of fabianism: a process which Miliband has amply documented.
But today the cardinal tenets of late fabianism have been
refuted by events: the bible of Crosland revisionism,
published in the mid-fifties, has dated more than any

other important work of socialist analysis published in Britain in the last fifty years. This means that Labour as a *movement*, as opposed to Labour as a potential government, can only exist on the basis of other doctrines, altogether more radical. The very pluralism involved in a federal structure becomes an advantage to socialists, since the integrating force of dogma has rotted away.

However, if this scenario is plausible, where must socialists engage themselves? There can hardly be a moment's doubt. Another Labour Government offers socialists the chance to do well the work which they botched last time: to force the imposition of socialist policies, or to isolate and defeat those who oppose them. While external critics might aid in this process, in its essentials it will either be an inside job or it won't get done. And if it *is* done, it will still imply the creation of a *new* or renewed, Labour Party, a federation, an alliance of all who seek change. It will still imply nationwide political organisation, participation in elections, and all that this requires. No magic barricades will sweep it all away and inaugurate a promised utopia, no soviets will re-emerge in pristine order from the textbooks, and no self-appointed elects will impose their rigorous orthodoxies on stevedores and coal-miners, or even teachers and computer-programmers, simply because the politicians have failed again. The soviets, which might be desirable, to say nothing of the orthodoxies, which certainly would not, *could* arrive at hegemony: but only in defence of gains already made within the given constitutional order. And no such gains are imaginable without the engagement of the overwhelming majority of the people who will, in 1973 or 1974, be voting Labour yet again, in spite of all the exhortations to which they have been exposed from the socialist missionaries of the groupuscules.

That is the first question: any new socialist party would

be impotent unless it replicated the best features of the
old Labour Party. In countries where the unions were
themselves established by the pre-existing socialist parties,
and where political organisation has long taken priority
over union membership, such formulae do not necessarily
apply: but they do apply in Britain, in many of the
former white dominions, in Belgium, and probably,
as Trotsky and his followers thought, in the United
States.

The second question is obvious. If the object is to establish a real Labour Party, and if this object cannot be
achieved without the support of many of the present
components of the existing pseudo-Labour Party, where
can socialists direct their efforts but at that very Party?
They may join it, or they may be organised outside it, but
they cannot ignore it, and influence over its members
must be their constant preoccupation. And that is what
happens. Both the most serious 'revolutionary' groups,
which is to say the two which publish daily newspapers,
are highly concerned to develop their policies in a way
which makes them intelligible and acceptable to Labour
Party members. The rest of the left tends to thank its
lucky stars that the quite different items of ideological
baggage carried by these two groups makes their work
unconscionably difficult. But for those who do not stagger
under this weight, what possible alternative can offer
itself but that of campaigning to develop an explicitly
socialist tendency within the Party? And if one admits
such a tendency might be developed, who can say, in
advance, whether it would be containable? If the unions
decide to support real socialist options, why should the
socialists need to split away? While, if the campaign is
at a lower level, for an inclusive socialist organisation,
why should that campaign not be waged within the existing Party?

The change in the balance of forces in the movement

at large must ultimately be reflected in its political councils. When the time comes, if there is a candidate with the insight and skill to present a platform of socialist change, he is very likely to win. Such a candidate would need, then, to 'put up a big character poster, and call on the masses to bombard the headquarters'. The headquarters, it must be admitted, certainly deserve a pasting. Meantime, whatever else British socialists may be doing, whatever experiments they feel it meet to conduct, either in community action or trade union agitation, the one thing they should *not* do is to turn their backs on the official Labour Movement. I think history may well come to adjudge that its Cultural Revolution has already begun: but in any event, the climax of that process is still to come, and is most unlikely to be long delayed. The work will be arduous and intricate, daunting indeed. It will need all the socialist forces we can muster, and, indeed, it needs them now. It would be time enough to talk about defeat if the battle were over, assuming our victories left us time: but it is quite, quite wrong to concern ourselves with it now, as the battle-lines are just beginning to form.

First published in 1973

FOOTNOTES

1. Ralph Miliband: *Parliamentary Socialism*, Merlin Press, 1973 Postscript, p.372.
2. When the ILP seceded from the Labour Party, at a time when capitalism was in deep trouble, it had 16,700 members, many of whom were strategically well-placed in the Labour Movement. Its historian, R. E. Dowse, records that between July and November 1932 it dropped 203 branches out of 653. Even so, it

might have made a better showing if it had not severed all its connections with the Labour Party by refusing to pay political levy, cut off relations with the Co-operative Movement, and gravely weakened its position in the unions. As it turned out, the much weaker Communist Party was to prove the beneficiary of the split, largely because of its capacity to maintain an intransigent, if contradictory, policy. Cf. *Left in the Centre*, Longmans, 1966, pp. 185 et seq.

3. I have developed this argument with Bill Silburn, in *Poverty, the Forgotten Englishmen*, Penguin Books, 1970. See Chapter 11, pp.216-35.

4. Cf. *The May-day Manifesto*, edited by Raymond Williams, Penguin Books, 1968.

5. This was never clearer than in the argument about British entry to the European Economic Community. Not only did several dozen Labour MPs defy the Party's decisions with impunity, so that the sole casualty was as much a victim of his own innate arrogance as of any political reprisals, but all attempts at mobilization in the country proved completely vain. All the specific grievances which workers felt about the decision were left uncoordinated and isolated. On the issue of Value Added Tax, which raises the most crucial questions about the nature of exploitation, (*who* added *what* value?) a purely parliamentary confrontation was staged, even though a severe freeze on wages was in progress at a time when prices were supposed to be fixed.

6. It is quite possible that parliamentary styles of government could be abrogated by the Right, given a continuation of present economic and social unease over any prolonged period. But unless this happens, workers will still continually turn to Parliament for any redress to their felt grievances: and in the event that any serious socialist reform programme is ever presented to the electorate working-people will find their aspirations under the same attack which is then mounted on parliamentary institutions. Short of a "cold" counter-revolution, if soviets were ever to emerge in Britain, it would be in defence of the right of Parliament to assert its alleged prerogatives, rather than as abstractly desirable bodies. In spite of the reservations of the far left about events in Chile, it still seems very possible that we shall see some such pattern emerge in that country.

7. *New Left Review*, No. 75, 1972.

8. Published as a Spokesman Pamphlet, No. 31, 1972.

9. Cf. Ernest Mandel: *Europe and America*, New Left Books, 1970, pp.40-60.

10. Cf. Andrée Hoyles: interview with Michel Rocard, in *The Spokesman*, nos. 13-14, 1971, pp.27-46.

11. Cf. Lelio Basso: A New Socialist Party, in *International Socialist Journal*, no. 2, 1964, pp.161-73.

12. Cf. Andrée Hoyles, The Occupation of Factories in France: May 1968, in *The Trade Union Register, 1969*, Merlin Press, 1969, pp.243-95, especially pp.287-8. Subsequently published as a separate book under the title *Imagination in Power*, Spokesman Books, 1973.

Afterword

The amount of water which has gone under the bridges since these papers were first published varies: several high floods have passed since 1967, a little more than a drought-trickle since 1976. It is therefore not easy to update the whole range of arguments which have been outlined above. A few salient issues, however, do require notice.

On the international plane, most socialists would recognise that a great victory and a great defeat have taken place during the span of years in question.

In Vietnam, the arrival in Saigon of the forces of the National Liberation Front, and the end of a third of a century of fighting with the total discomfiture of the Americans, did significantly tilt the balance of forces in the world, to the considerable disadvantage of Empire.

The consequences in the United States itself were tumultuous, unleashing the whole savage argument of Watergate, and, as a result, prising open the filing cabinets of the C.I.A. and other American intelligence services so that a couple of decades of frenetic subversion throughout the third world became the object of belated public scrutiny. In the colonial world, dominoes fell almost immediately, not in Bangkok, as had been feared by the State Department, but in Mozambique, Angola and Guinea-Bissau. Today Zimbabwe and South Africa are really in the 'front line', and there can be little doubt that new and far-reaching changes will soon take place.

The lesson of these events is direct and obvious. Colonial wars of liberation will continue to erupt, and some, at least, have prospects of success. Does this mean that Lin Piao was right, and that the transition to socialism, world-wide, results from the fact that 'the countryside encircles the town'? I do not think so.

First of all, socialism will never know its real potential until it begins to be applied in one or more of the most economically advanced countries: and whatever experiments may be made in direct democracy in the poor nations, socialist democracy proper requires a cultured and well-integrated working-class movement, and a high proportion of industrialisation, so that manual and mental employees, taken together, can constitute the overwhelming majority of the population. This implies that the experience of revolution in Black Africa or South East Asia, however important and encouraging, will not constitute a model for socialist organisation in the former metropolitan centres. Whilst the attention of radicals, reformers, socialists and, of course, black people, in the U.S.A. or Great Britain will no doubt rivet itself firmly on Southern Africa during the next half decade or so, this will be the result of felt moral affinities rather than enlistment in the same army: freedom in South Africa still lies at the end of a different road to that which leads to freedom in the dominant half-democracies.

The major defeat, which also points this lesson is, of course, that in Chile. Militarist usurpation, terror and brutal repression have resulted in the death of President Allende and his brave attempt in peaceful socialist reform. Allende's Chile was without political prisoners, without governmental censorship, without the slightest inhibition of the received democratic processes. Today, those who worked to apply these processes to the pursuit of reform are either dead, or exiled, or fugitives within their own miserably unhappy country.

Does this mean that the very idea of peaceful socialist

development is Utopian, as so many young people are now apparently convinced? I think not. Quite apart from the arguments which have been advanced about the particular Chilean social structure, or about alleged errors of judgement by the Popular Unity Government, all of which are lengthily discussed elsewhere, I believe that the central question was posed, and needs an answer, outside Chile.

If international subversion is the response of beleaguered capitalism to all attempts at socialist democracy, and it seems evident that this is so, then the only possible socialist response is international solidarity. If Pinochet's Government could not have been strangled at birth by international action, it could have been harassed and attacked on all sides, by all the devices of boycott and ostracism which have ever been invented in free trade unions. Such a response, has, several times, *nearly* happened here or there. For it to *actually* happen in a co-ordinated way would be for it to take on lethal force, if not as antidote to Pinochet himself, at any rate to his would-be successors. But we shall not solve the logistics of this problem without discovering the way to revive, in the international organisations of labour, the catholic, all-embracing spirit and energy which gave birth to them.

This task is a formidable one. Because it is my conviction that the key to its resolution is the rediscovery of the vision of democratic socialism, meaning socialist democracy, I think that the mistakes in this little book may be forgiven, if only it sees straight about the main issue.

As for the fate of poor England, the Labour Party has, since the last paper in this book was written, given rise to a remarkable debate, and the 1974 Labour Governments *have*, in the main, followed all the precedents of their forerunners. Yet, paradoxically, the more openly incompetent that Government policy becomes, the more vital and alive the frustrated membership of the Governmental

Party appears to be. This state of affairs cannot, presumably, continue for long, and it will be interesting to see how it resolves itself.

Ken Coates

Index

SOME OTHER SPOKESMAN TITLES

THE NEW WORKER COOPERATIVES

ed. Ken Coates

Cloth £5.50
Paper £2.25

INDUSTRIAL DEMOCRACY IN GREAT BRITAIN:
A Book of Readings and Witnesses
For Workers' Control

ed. Ken Coates and Tony Topham

Vol I   Schools for Democrats
Paper £1.05

Vol II   Shop Stewards and Workers' Control, 1910–1964
Paper £1.25

Vol III   Industrial Democracy and Nationalisation
Paper £0.95

'This anthology is a major publishing event, one to be very thankful for.'—*John Hughes*

SABOTAGE: A Study in Industrial Conflict

by Geoff Brown

Cloth £8.50

ARE LOW WAGES INEVITABLE?

ed. Frank Field

Cloth £4.75
Paper £1.95

THE IDIOT TEACHER

by Gerard Holmes

'The schools are now to re-think their achievements and activities. I hope they will not ignore the discoveries of Teddy O'Neil earlier this century.'
—*Dr. V. P. Houghton of The Open University*

Paper £1.95